Bedroom & Bath Storage

By the Editors of Sunset Books
and Sunset Magazine

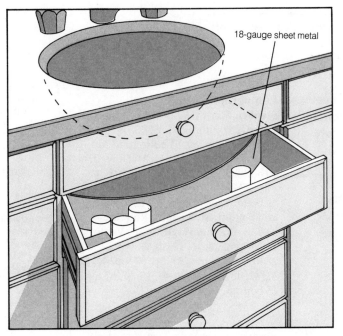

18-gauge sheet metal

*Drawers with rounded backs make the most of undersink
space (see page 55).*

Lane Publishing Co.
Menlo Park, California

¾" plywood

2-by cherry

Underbed storage opens up floor space in a child's room (see page 25).

Book Editors
Helen Sweetland
Ginger Smith Bate

Contributing Editors
Scott Atkinson
Fran Feldman

Design
Roger Flanagan
Kathy Avanzino Barone

Photo Stylist
JoAnn Masaoka

Illustrations
Rik Olson

We gratefully acknowledge the following businesses for their help with material for this book: Crate & Barrel, Hold Everything, Just Closets, and Stacks & Stacks.

We also extend special thanks to Marianne Lipanovich for scouting many of the photo locations.

Photographers
Stephen Marley: 9 bottom, 11 top, 13, 19 top, 23 bottom, 24, 36, 38, 39 top, 45 top, 58, 59 top, 60, 61 bottom, 63 top right, 65 top, 67, 70. **Jack McDowell:** 10 bottom, 12, 15, 19 bottom, 20 bottom, 37 bottom, 39 bottom, 43 bottom, 45 bottom, 59 bottom, 62, 63 top left and bottom, 64, 66 right. **Rob Super:** 34 bottom. **Tom Wyatt:** 9 top, 10 top, 11 bottom, 14, 16, 17, 18, 20 top, 21, 22, 23 top, 33, 34 top, 35 top, 37 top, 40, 41, 42, 43 top, 44, 46, 47, 48, 57, 61 top, 65 bottom, 66 left, 68, 69, 71.

Cover: Dressing area off the master bedroom and adjacent to the master bath offers lots of convenient—and carefully organized—storage. A stack of shallow drawers holds lingerie and accessories. Below is a hamper ready to catch clothing or linens from the bath. Nine pull-out shelves house shoes and sweaters, with room for more above. Long apparel hangs from the single rod at left; shorter items fit on double rods at right. For more on this storage system, turn to page 42. Architect: Mark Hajjar. Photo styling by JoAnn Masaoka. Photographed by Tom Wyatt.

Sunset Books
    Editor: David E. Clark
    Managing Editor: Elizabeth L. Hogan

First printing August 1988

Contents

Careful planning turns a simple wall closet into a highly efficient storage system (see page 32).

Bedroom Storage

Because space is at a premium in most homes today, bedrooms must perform more than one role—and still remain restful oases where the cares of the day can be left behind. The challenge is learning how to combine many functions in one space, without ending up with uncontrolled clutter.

The first step is to take an inventory, not only of the items in the room but also of the activities normally carried on there. Is this where you like to read and listen to music? Do you normally do your ironing in this room? Would your home computer be more convenient to use if it were in the bedroom? Is this where your children enjoy playing? Once you have a clear idea of what functions you want the room to serve, you'll be able to organize it to work for you.

Look at your room with fresh eyes, starting with the largest space-gobbler of all—the bed. Make it serve as a major storage spot by surrounding it with a functional and roomy headboard system, by fitting it with underbed storage drawers, or even by adding a storage compartment at the foot. If your ceiling is high, you may want to consider building a sleeping loft, or perhaps raising the bed off the floor. You can even make the bed disappear into the wall, Murphy-bed fashion.

Next, think about the amenities that make the room restful and relaxing—books and magazines for bedside reading, a television and perhaps a stereo system for entertainment, extra pillows and quilts for comfort. Shelves, hollow headboards, linen closets, nightstands, and drawers can put all these items within easy reach.

Finally, you're ready to choose—or design—your own storage units or systems. What you select will depend not only on what you need to store but also on your taste and budget. Perhaps you like the informal look of simple bins or baskets. Or you may prefer antique furniture and closed cabinetry. In any case, efficiency should be your goal.

In this chapter, you'll see how some homeowners organized their rooms, and you'll find some easy projects you can make yourself with basic skills and simple tools. Whatever your requirements and taste, you'll discover a bounty of good ideas to stimulate your creativity.

Storage Chests

Custom designs offer built-in convenience

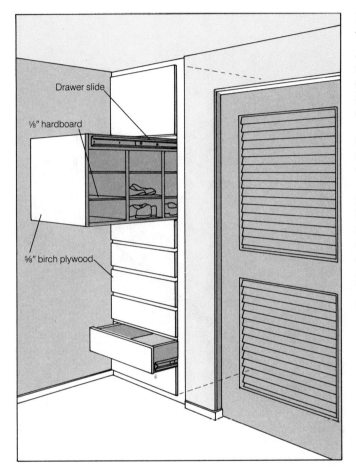

Drawer slide

⅛" hardboard

⅝" birch plywood

Built-in chest saves valuable floor space

A built-in chest that replaces a freestanding bureau can save several feet of floor space in your bedroom. Set into a corner beside a wide closet, this chest leaves room for a larger bed or perhaps a desk and chair. For optimum storage, the drawers are as deep as the closet.

The door and drawer fronts can be cut from one sheet of ⅝-inch birch plywood for a continuous grain pattern. For a finished appearance, band the edges with ⅜-inch alder, walnut, or oak, glued into place.

The vertical supports in the pigeonhole pull-out are made from ⅝-inch plywood; the bases are ⅛-inch hardboard. Use full-extension drawer slides available from cabinet suppliers or well-stocked lumberyards for support and easy access to the compartments. The edges of the drawers are routed for ease in opening. Attach the door for the top cabinet with self-closing concealed hinges. Architect: Rod Terry.

Storage bench

Like a stack of increasingly bigger boxes, this storage bench is deeper at the top for accessibility, shallower at the base for extra toe space.

Horizontal 1 by 4s wrapping the sides and front are glued and nailed to vertical 1 by 8s; these are notched so each of the front 1 by 4s cantilevers about 2 inches over the one below it. For ventilation, leave a 1-inch gap between each 1 by 4. At the wall, the 1 by 4s are glued and nailed to vertical 1 by 2s screwed to wall studs. The bench rests on a recessed 2 by 2 base.

To strengthen the lid, glue 1 by 4s to ⅛-inch tempered hardboard and add tapered 2 by 2s to the underside. Cut the lid's edges at an angle. Designer: John Parsons.

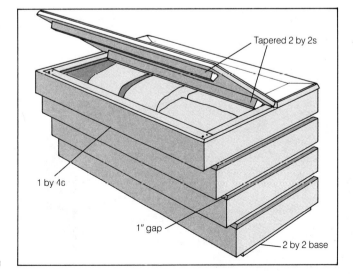

Tapered 2 by 2s

1 by 4s

1" gap

2 by 2 base

Bedside Storage Systems

Four easy-to-build units that you can use separately
—or in various combinations—to boost bedside storage

Build just one component or build them all

A small bedroom, especially one that doubles as a home office or den, is a storage challenge. One way to maximize bedroom space is to make the bed itself as storage-efficient as possible.

The system shown here gives you three units for stowing things—a headboard, a nightstand, and a foot-of-the-bed chest. Just choose the components that fit your storage needs, your room layout, and your taste. Alter the dimensions as you wish. The components are described in detail below and at the top of the facing page. (For drawer-building tips, see page 77.)

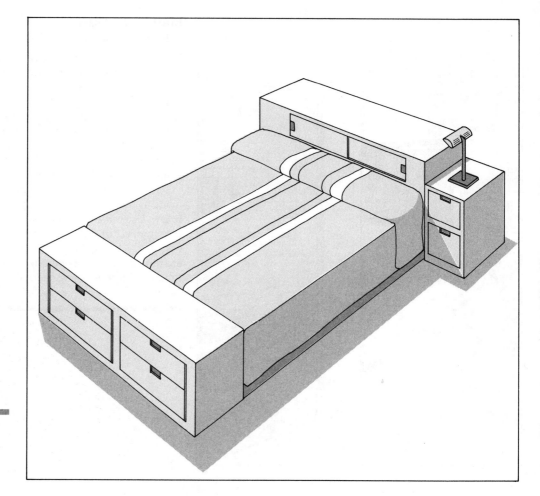

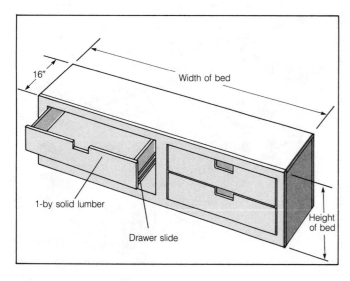

16"

Width of bed

1-by solid lumber

Drawer slide

Height of bed

The foot-of-the-bed chest

A low chest of drawers at the foot of a full-size bed has nearly the same storage capacity as a traditional bedroom bureau, yet it's not nearly as bulky. It can also double as a bench or television shelf.

You can buy a unit built especially for the foot of the bed; or try one designed for a different purpose (such as storing engineers' maps and blueprints).

To put together a chest like the one shown, build a frame from ¾-inch plywood and 1-by solid lumber; then install four custom-made drawers on standard slides. Make the chest the same height and width as your bed and approximately 16 inches deep.

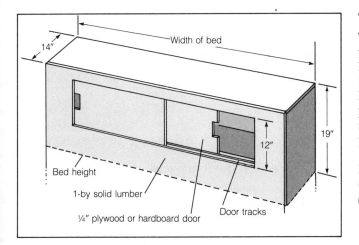

Width of bed
14"
19"
12"
Bed height
1-by solid lumber
¼" plywood or hardboard door
Door tracks

The headboard

The simple unit shown at left has a storage compartment with handy sliding doors to hide clutter. The portion of the headboard above the mattress should be approximately 19 inches high and 14 inches deep; the width and overall height of the headboard will be determined by the size of your bed. Sheets, blankets, pillows, and bedspreads alter measurements, so it's wise to measure when these are in place.

Build the headboard from ¾-inch plywood and 1-by solid lumber. Use ¼-inch plywood or hardboard for the sliding doors, and install plastic, wood, or metal door tracks.

The nightstand

Two storage compartments are stacked inside this compact unit (see at right). The top one is a cubbyhole with a hinged, drop-down door in front; below it is a roomy drawer.

The nightstand shown here is approximately 12 inches wide, 14 inches deep, and 26 inches high; you can adjust these dimensions to suit your own needs.

Build the unit from ¾-inch plywood and 1-by solid lumber. Buy a ready-made drawer—or build your own—and install it on standard drawer slides.

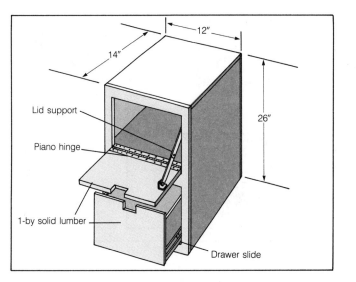

12"
14"
26"
Lid support
Piano hinge
1-by solid lumber
Drawer slide

Easy-to-build storage headboard

With two storage levels, this headboard has plenty of room for bulky pillows and comforters, and even hard-to-store sports equipment. What's more, the door of the upper compartment doubles as a slanting backrest.

The depth of the unit is 24 inches. Make the headboard 12 inches higher and a little wider than your bed. The backrest/door slants at a 75° angle.

Build the headboard from ¾-inch plywood. Before assembly, cut a door out of each side piece. Assemble the pieces, nail 1 by 3 cleats to the inside of the headboard to hold the interior shelf, and attach the large door with a piano hinge. Attach the side doors with hinges and add door pulls and magnetic catches.

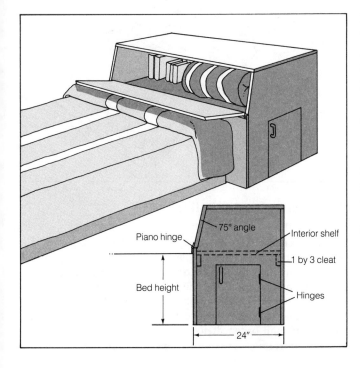

75° angle
Piano hinge
Interior shelf
1 by 3 cleat
Bed height
Hinges
24"

Underbed Storage

If the area under your bed collects nothing but dust, add chests or pull-outs—or a custom-designed storage platform—to utilize that wealth of wasted space

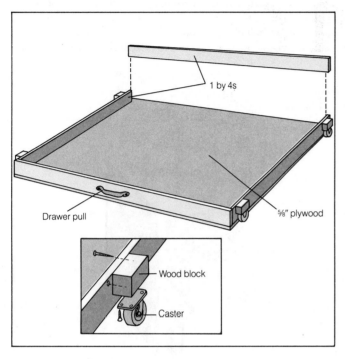

1 by 4s

Drawer pull

⅝" plywood

Wood block

Caster

Make your own roll-out drawers

Even a standard metal bedframe can accommodate underbed storage. To build a simple drawer, fasten 1 by 4 strips to the edges of a ⅝-inch plywood bottom (as shown). Then add the wood blocks and casters (remember to allow an inch or so for clearance—more for thick carpeting) and attach a drawer pull. A plywood lid will keep items dust-free—but you'll have to pull the drawer out completely for access or hinge the lid in the center.

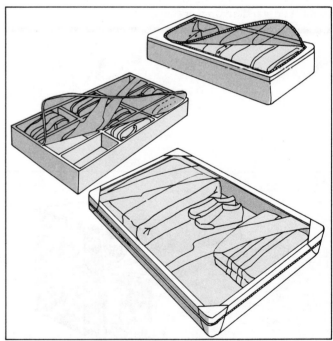

Custom bed holds roll-around cart

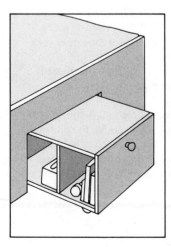

Designing a new bed? Consider leaving space for a handy roll-around cart with storage compartments, like the one shown here. Tucked away, the unit blends in with the rest of the underbed cabinetry. Pulled out, the cart doubles as a nightstand or breakfast-in-bed table.

Ready-made containers slide under standard bedframes

Trays and chests made expressly for underbed storage are commercially available in plastic, wood, or cardboard. Many have dividers; most have lids or see-through vinyl covers. These inexpensive storage aids are perfect for shoes, out-of-season clothing, and bed linens. Look for them in the notions sections of department stores or in mail-order catalogs.

Modular pieces that fit your style

Modules that can be arranged under and around your bed can give you plenty of extra stowing space—even in small bedrooms. The drawer under this bed rolls out when you need it. Such drawers are available in various widths and depths. The three-drawer chests on either side of the headboard are separate units, too. Design: The Minimal Space.

Bedframe features double-decker drawers

Two levels of drawers are built into this striking bedframe, which is coated with glossy black lacquer. The upper level is perfect for sweaters and lingerie; the lower level is roomy enough for extra bedding. Heavy-duty metal slides let the drawers open and close smoothly. Architect: Wendell Lovett. Interior design: Suzanne Braddock.

Headboard Systems

Built-in or freestanding, headboard systems
offer bedside convenience

Floral reflections

Mirrors over the bed and closets open up this very functional headboard system, reflecting light and enlarging the bedroom. Just under the bedside lamps are built-in nightstands that offer storage beside the bed. Tall cupboards—one with drawers, the other with shelves—hold clothing and extra pillows. Interior design: Patricia Whitt Designs.

Keeping a low profile

When you need storage space around your bed but you don't have room for an elaborate wall system, consider this sleek design. The headboard proper has two bins for pillows and extra bedding. The side sections store books and other bedside necessities; doors fold down to function as nightstands. The headboard's slanted front provides gentle support for television watching or reading. Design: The Minimal Space.

Headboard appropriates a whole wall

Commodious and versatile, this headboard wall system provides generous storage for everything from books to clothing to Christmas tree lights, while catering to bedside needs. Tucked into its custom-fitted alcove, the head of the bed has behind-the-pillows storage and a ledge for midnight snacks. For reading, there's ample light from the recessed fixtures above. Design: Euro-design, Ltd.

Bedside office

Floor-to-ceiling headboard wall system in this bedroom is all business, from the spacious cupboards and drawers for clothes and bedding to the hanging-file drawer beside the bed for papers and records. Recessed downlights above boost the illumination provided by the swing-arm fixtures. Interior design: Ruth Soforenko Associates.

Room-dividing Headboards

A two-faced approach to both spatial and storage needs

Floating island in a tranquil setting

In this pretty, pale bedroom, the bed takes center stage—it's a serene island of comfort as well as hard-working storage. Its massive yet sleek headboard is the focal point, partitioning the room into sleeping and dressing areas. On the sleeping side, almost hidden behind the bed pillows, cabinet doors cover storage crannies for bedside necessities; above them, an airy alcove more than accommodates reading lamps, books, a clock-radio, and a pretty plant. On the opposite side, the headboard serves up a dozen drawers, topped with a mirrored niche for toiletries and a jewelry box. Architect: Phoebe T. Wall.

Extra warmth on one side, extra storage on the other

In a bedroom of generous size, this freestanding fireplace wall separates a cozy sitting area from the sleeping quarters. On the headboard side of the wall, bookshelves surround a center panel that offers swing-arm lamps—and plenty of space to prop pillows—for bedtime reading. Architects: The Bumgardner Architects.

Handsome, clever, and capacious

More than compensating for the bedroom's single small closet, this vast bedframe-headboard-wardrobe unit also creates a private dressing corridor behind the bed. In front, tawny oak shelves climb nearly to the ceiling, framing an upholstered backrest. In back, the same rich oak forms a capacious set of cabinets and drawers. Design: The Butt Joint.

Hideaway Beds

For small bedrooms, guest bedrooms, double-duty bedrooms—
sleeping facilities that literally come out of the woodwork

Sleepy? Just pull down the wall

Mr. Murphy's popular invention of 1905 swung down out of a closet. Today's versions, which operate in a similar fashion, are just as likely to pull down from a recess in a wall, like the one shown here, as from a closet. Gas springs (pneumatic closers) at the head of the bed allow for easy lifting and lowering. Legs at the foot provide needed support and stability.

Other space-saving features of the handsome wall system include a fold-down bedside table on one side and a pull-out work surface on the other. Recessed downlights above the bed are controlled by a switch just above the pillows. To make your own Murphy bed, turn to pages 26–27. Interior design: Legallet-Trinkner Design Associates. Furniture design: Eurodesign, Ltd.

Daytime seating becomes nighttime bedding

Nestled in a nook of a none-too-spacious cedar cabin, the built-in bench pictured above gets in nobody's way during the day. And when it's bedtime, the base and cushion fold out separately, transforming the seating area into the double bed shown on the left. Separate supports for the sleeping platform are kept in a drawer beneath the bench during the day. Architects: Larsen, Lagerquist & Morris.

Double-duty Bedrooms

Managing the paraphernalia when sleeping quarters
share space with hobbies or homework

Wraparound cabinetry creates office/guestroom

Built-in cabinets, counters, and shelves convert this small room into an efficient family computer center and office. When the sofa bed is opened up, the room becomes a guest bedroom; there's drawer space for clothing and cleverly concealed pull-out shelves on either side of the sofa for bedside storage. Interior design: Lynn Williams of The French Connection.

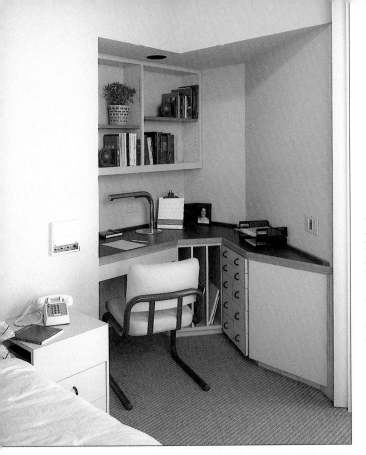

Corner cutout for paperwork in privacy

For book-balancing or tax forms, thank-you notes or PTA flyers, epic poems or crossword puzzles, a small home office certainly aids achievement. But where to put it? Most homes nowadays lack spare rooms that aren't already reserved for the television or visiting relatives.

As this situation shows, a bedroom corner may provide the ideal location—out of traffic's way and relatively private. This office is neatly tucked into an alcove originally intended as a closet. The angles of the desk allow for leg room and a bank of drawers, as well as vertical slots large enough for sketch pads and blueprints; the wraparound desktop offers ample work space. Overhead, a small bookcase completes the corner. Architect: David Jeremiah Hurley. Interior design: Jois.

Camera cache in a closet

Most of us connect closets with clothing. Naturalists may think first of moths, psychiatrists and genealogists of skeletons. But to an enthusiastic photographer, the closet in a spare bedroom can serve quite a different purpose: safely storing all the delicate and valuable apparatus of his craft. Here, floor-to-ceiling adjustable shelves behind bifold closet doors keep cameras and gear in tidy, easily accessible order. There's even room on the closet floor for a small refrigerator for film. Closet interior: Just Closets.

Bedroom Wall Systems

Cabinets, drawers, open shelves keep your private world in order

A wall of cabinets and drawers

With a wall system such as this one, nothing need ever be out of place in this bedroom! At the very top are bins that swing down to collect seldom-used blankets and sports equipment. Just below, doors open to reveal vinyl-coated wire baskets, as shown, or adjustable shelves. One unit houses the television. At the bottom are a dozen and a half drawers for sweaters, shirts, and accessories. Track lighting illuminates the scene. Design and construction: Robert Nyden.

A place for everything and . . .

From books to the telephone to towels for an adjoining bath, this headboard system holds it all. There's a pull-out drawer under the bed for bulky sweaters and a roomy bin behind the pillows. The cabinet door even pulls down to become an instant nightstand, as shown at left.

Systems such as this one can be tailored to your own needs, whether you're storing books, bedding, or belts. Design: Eurodesign, Ltd.

That's entertainment!

On display here are some of the essentials of a bedroom entertainment center: stereo components, a library of record albums, and several shelves of books. For stow-away storage, this attractive wooden wall system also offers drawers and more drawers, cabinets and more cabinets. Three cubbyholes along the countertop have the same kind of covering found on rolltop desks. For ideas on storing the bedroom TV—another entertainment essential—turn to pages 20 and 21. Architect: Robert C. Peterson.

In a nutshell—it's natty

Open the big doors in this wall unit, and what do you find but a handy small-scale closet. Crisp shirts on a pull-out rod line up along its center, while neckties hang neatly from racks placed high on either cabinet door. With nary an inch of wall space wasted, cabinets and drawers abound, surrounding the counter and recessed mirror. Design: Euro-design, Ltd.

Television Storage

Keeping the set out of sight when it's out of mind

Rolltop reviewing stand

Early in the morning or late at night, this television, situated in the "adults only" corner of the master bedroom, emerges from behind a rolltop door and slides out of its alcove on a shelf fitted with a swiveling platform. A tiled fireplace, a wet bar with storage, and a small refrigerator concealed behind cabinet doors below the sink complete the scene. Architect: Victor Conforti.

Sharing space with the shirts

The owner of this handsome, custom-built armoire can watch the morning news as he selects a shirt for the day. The television is bolted securely to a swivel-topped pull-out shelf, so it can be turned or brought forward for easier viewing. But when TV time is over and the armoire doors are closed, there's no hint of the screen—or the shirts.

Even in antique storage pieces, there are often nooks and crannies that can be used for television storage; an antique hideaway is shown on page 23. Interior design: Anona Colvin.

Elevated viewing, window seat sound

The owners of this bedroom located their television high above their closet so they could comfortably watch while lying in bed. The controls are, of course, remote. Stereo components and speakers fit in small alcoves on both sides of the window seat; the speakers can be angled toward the seat or turned to project into the bedroom. Interior design: Ruth Soforenko Associates.

One set does double duty

Though located in the sitting room of this two-level master bedroom suite, this television is also visible from the bedroom up the stairs to the right, thanks to a pull-out shelf and swiveling platform. At the end of the wall unit is a linen closet pictured on page 65. Architect: Mark Hajjar. Interior design: Patricia Whitt Designs.

Antique Storage Furniture

Yesterday's chests and dressers still hold their own as storage units

Treasured chests for bedroom storage

This bedroom's storage begins with a closet for clothes that must be hung, then expands storage space with a graceful armoire, a handsome wood-trimmed trunk, and a refurbished tool chest made fresh with paint and stencils.

An antique quilt hangs on a wall hoop, while two others see service on crisp winter evenings.

Victorian hideaway for books, TV

Last century's clothes-keepers can be refurbished to suit contemporary tastes and to hold one of this century's most popular inventions. This richly carved Victorian armoire, American-made of oak, was stripped, bleached, and finally waxed to show off its natural golden color. The interior has been lined, and the doors upholstered, in a fabric that matches the bedroom wallpaper. Finally, a swivel-topped, pull-out plywood tray was added to hold a television set. Interior design: Ruth Soforenko Associates.

For the new generation

Tall wooden wardrobe holds the tiny clothes of the newest entry in the family line. Blankets for the crib fit into the drawer at the bottom. Wicker hampers that may once have served for day trips or afternoon picnics hold little shirts or a few days' supply of diapers.

The rocking horse, wicker rocker, and brass crib echo the traditional theme.

Children's Rooms

Storing toys and clothes so they're easy to reach,
easy to put away, and easy on the eyes

A second level and lots of drawers

This bed-loft system adds several feet of level surface for
games and projects in this child's room. Combine that with
almost a dozen drawers and some shelves, and you have
the potential for order—even in a small bedroom. Design:
Adventures in Space.

Sit and store with handy shelves and drawers

Shelves beside this window seat and drawers underneath
put toys and clothes at arm's reach. Bright pillows and
cuddly buddies invite lingering. Design: Sharon Kasser,
Distinctive Interiors.

3/4" plywood

2-by cherry

Handsome chest bed is a real worker

For tucking away toys, clothing, and sleepy children, consider a chest bed with generous drawer space. In addition to the drawers, there's a deep bin in the back for linens. To get to the bin, you lift up the twin-size mattress and open the lid.

The pieces are cut from good-looking Baltic birch plywood where appearance counts; where it doesn't, less expensive shop-grade plywood is used. Make the rails from solid cherry and use 1/4-inch tempered hardboard for the bin and drawer bottoms. The lid under the mattress is attached with a long piano hinge. Design: Robert Zumwalt.

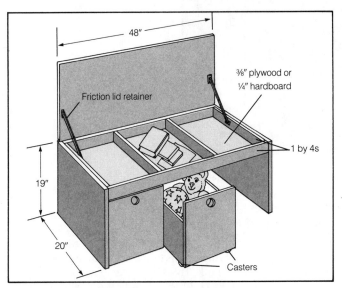

48"

Friction lid retainer

3/8" plywood or 1/4" hardboard

1 by 4s

19"

20"

Casters

Drawing desk holds a row of rolling toy bins

With the lid down, a toy bin or two pulled out, and a small chair pulled up, this handy unit serves as a drawing desk. But when playtime is over, the toy bins slide under the desktop to form a single, compact storage unit. Desk sides, back, and lid are built from 3/4-inch plywood; the bottom of the divided tray is made of 3/8-inch plywood or 1/4-inch hardboard; and the tray frame is built from fir 1 by 4s. The unit illustrated is 19 inches high, 20 inches deep, and 48 inches wide, but you can adjust these dimensions to suit your child's needs.

Assemble the desk with glue and woodscrews or finishing nails. Attach the swing-up lid with a piano hinge, and add a lid support (or chain) at each end. Depending on the dimensions of your unit, the drawers of an old file cabinet might furnish ready-to-use bins (just add casters); or make your own bins from plywood. Finish the desk and bins with bright-colored enamel.

Versatility with building blocks

Storage modules do more than organize mountains of playthings. They can be combined to form desks, platform beds, room dividers, and wall systems. You can buy ready-made modules made from wood, particleboard, or plastic—or you can build your own.

Construct your modules from 3/4-inch plywood suitable for painting. A convenient size for each module is 16 inches square; for compatibility, make rectangular ones 16 by 16 by 32 inches. Add shelves (they double as vertical dividers when you rearrange the modules), hinged doors, or even simple drawers; use wood molding or veneer tape to hide the plywood edges. Finish with enamel. If you stack several modules, be sure to bolt them to the wall or floor—or to each other—for stability.

Murphy Beds

Fold them up when they're not in use

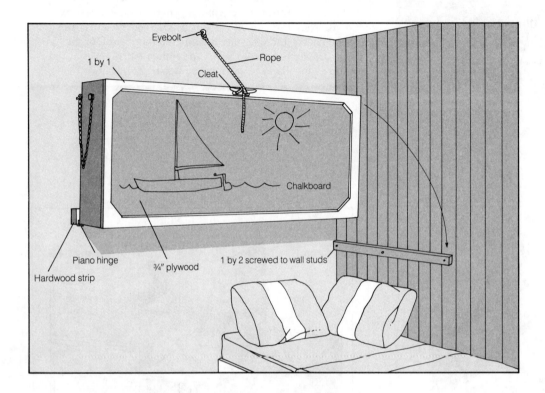

Eyebolt

Rope

Cleat

1 by 1

Chalkboard

Piano hinge

Hardwood strip

¾" plywood

1 by 2 screwed to wall studs

Chalk one up for Murphy

Since 1905, Murphy beds have been folded up or slid into closets, quickly emptying rooms of wrinkled linens and at least 18 square feet of bulk. This simple version of the Murphy, designed for a child's room, is both a top bunk and a chalkboard.

Its base and sides are a shallow box made from ¾-inch plywood. The good face of the base plywood is placed down to form the bed's underside and is painted with chalkboard paint. A 1 by 1, fastened (either nailed and glued, or screwed) to the sides, supports the base, and plywood triangles at the corners add strength. The frame can be designed to hold either a cot- or standard-size mattress.

The bed pivots down on a 6-foot piano hinge, screwed to a hardwood strip anchored to wall studs. A heavy chain, securely fastened at one end to a wall stud or ceiling joist and, at the other, to an end of the bunk, holds the bed level when it's folded down. At the head of the bunk, a 1 by 2 is screwed to the wall studs, further supporting the bed's weight. A rope wraps around a boat cleat to hold the bunk in its raised position.

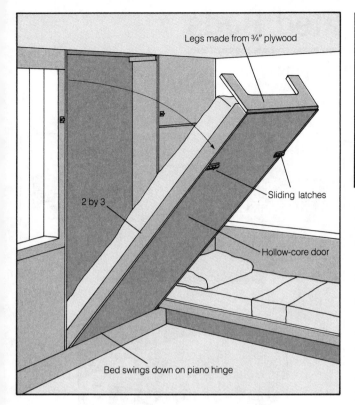

Legs made from ¾" plywood

Sliding latches

2 by 3

Hollow-core door

Bed swings down on piano hinge

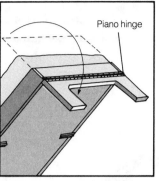

Piano hinge

Now you see it, now you don't

When guests spend the night, you can create an instant bedroom with a wall bed. Several manufacturers make them and stores that specialize in furnishings for apartments and small spaces carry them.

But if you want to make your own version of a Murphy bed, consider this one. The base is a hollow-core door onto which 2 by 3s are glued to form a shallow box. (You can also use ⅝-inch plywood as a base.) A 6-inch mattress is secured to the frame by woven straps.

The frame swings up on a piano hinge into a 9½-inch-deep well and is held in place by sliding latches. When it's pulled down for use, legs swing down on a piano hinge to support the foot of the bed. The legs, cut from ¾-inch plywood, are curved to allow for kickspace at the foot of the bed.

This version of the Murphy is for one person only, and the mattress is lightweight foam. For a larger bed with a standard mattress, you'll need heavy counter-spring hardware, rather than a piano hinge, to handle the weight.

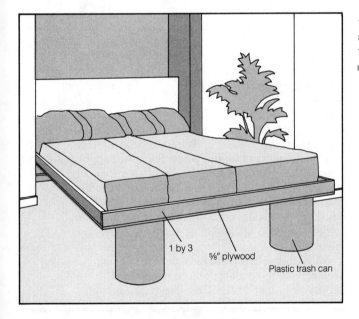

1 by 3   ⅝" plywood

Plastic trash can

Queen-size bed stores in closet

The platform of this queen-size bed, fitted with a foam mattress, rests on large cylinders that are actually sturdy plastic trash cans. The platform is made from ⅝-inch plywood and 1 by 3 lumber. A spring-loaded roller catch secures the bed at the top.

Sleeping Lofts & Elevated Beds

If your bedroom has a high ceiling, elevate your sleeping area
to open up storage or living space below

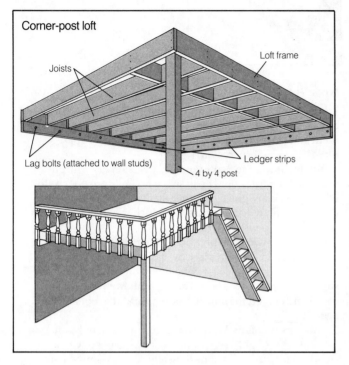

Corner-post loft

Joists
Loft frame
Lag bolts (attached to wall studs)
Ledger strips
4 by 4 post

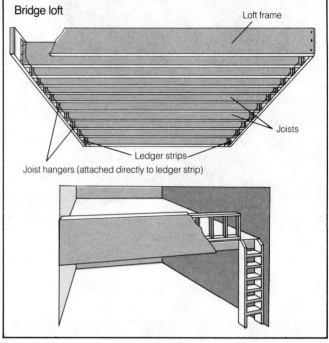

Bridge loft

Loft frame
Joists
Ledger strips
Joist hangers (attached directly to ledger strip)

Lofty ideas

Lofts are simply elevated platforms that add floor space
—and visual interest—to a room. They're especially useful in studio apartments (renters should check with the
landlord before building, of course) and in bedrooms
that double as work or entertainment centers.

Ceiling height, obviously, is a critical factor. As a
practical guide, consider $6\frac{1}{2}$ feet the minimum headroom needed for standing below a loft, and $4\frac{1}{2}$ feet the
minimum headroom needed for sitting up in the bed
above. (But always check your local building codes; the
requirements for your area may be different.) Add
another foot for the structure of the loft itself, and you'll
find that you need a ceiling that's about 12 feet high. If
you have the 8-foot ceilings that are standard in so
many newer homes, you'll have to remove all or part of
the existing ceiling, or be content with the more "down-
to-earth" forms of underbed storage (see pages 8–9).

Two basic loft designs are illustrated here. The corner-
post loft is supported by a ledger strip on one wall and
two corner posts, or by ledger strips on two adjoining
walls and one corner post. The bridge loft touches three
adjoining walls and is supported by ledger strips on the
two opposing ones. A third type (not shown) is a free-

standing loft, which requires support posts on all four
corners with braces to prevent sway. But the freestanding
loft is not as sturdy as the other two, and it's more com-
plicated to build.

Once you've determined your design and dimensions, check them with your local building department.

Use structural fir for the loft frame and wall ledgers.
(Essentially, you're building a new floor and supporting
it above the existing one, so the size of your structural
lumber will depend on the number of feet the loft will
span. Check local codes.) You'll also need $\frac{3}{4}$-inch plywood for the loft floor, 4 by 4s of structural fir for any
corner support posts, and materials for a ladder and
safety rails.

You'll probably want to furnish your loft simply, in
keeping with its small scale. And remember that it's a
sleeping loft—not designed for heavy storage.

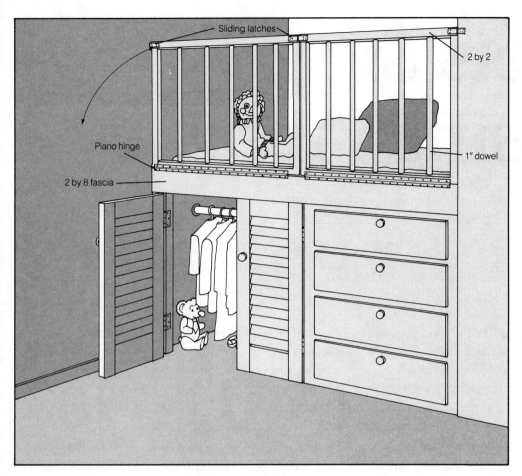

Sliding latches

2 by 2

Piano hinge

1" dowel

2 by 8 fascia

Sleep above, store below

This elevated crib-and-storage unit is just 5½ feet wide, yet handles several functions at once.

A frame of 2 by 6s, hung from the walls with joist hangers, supports a ⅝-inch-thick particleboard platform for a twin-size mattress (cut down to length). Mounted on the 2 by 8 fascia across the front are a pair of safety-rail gates made from 2 by 2s and 1-inch dowels. The gates pivot on piano hinges and fasten with spring-loaded sliding latches.

Drawers and a child-size closet under the crib provide convenient storage for clothing.

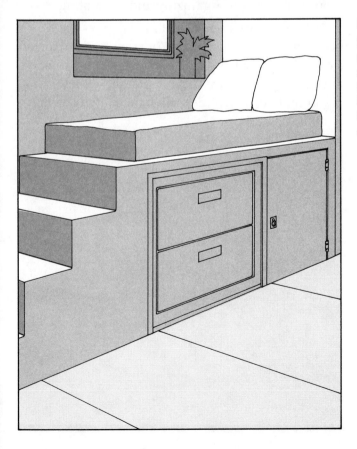

Storage base for twin-size bed

Stepped edge gives a sculptural look to this 4- by 8-foot sleeping platform. It's large enough for a twin-size mattress and high enough to accommodate a 2½-foot double-drawer filing cabinet. A cupboard adds additional storage space; fit it with pull-outs to make the space easily accessible. Architect: Franklin Israel.

Closets & Dressing Areas

Just about everyone would like to have an organized closet—one so well planned and tidy that a desired garment could be easily found, and in sparkling condition, rather than crumpled from crowding. In this chapter, we present many good ideas for turning a cluttered, messy closet into one that easily accommodates your wardrobe.

Most closets are either the roomy, walk-in type or the shallow but lengthy wall type. Both have their advantages. In general, people with large wardrobes prefer the walk-in closet, simply because it holds more. But with good space planning and double-decker closet rods, a wall closet can often accommodate the same-size collection of clothing. Shelves, drawers, pull-out bins, and racks, such as those pictured on the following pages, can make either closet more space-efficient and organized.

Before you purchase any storage aids or design a new closet, take careful stock of what you need to store. Start by eliminating clothing that you don't—or won't—wear. Then put your clothing into categories and take some measurements. Find out just how much room you need to store your shoes, or the height at which dresses should be hung so their hems won't drag on the floor. Then you'll be able to determine if your present closet—with the addition of another rod or two, some shelves, and a few racks and hooks—will give you sufficient space.

If necessary, consider ways to enlarge your present closet, or think about where you can build a new one. On the following pages, we present suggestions for temporary, or movable, closets, as well as instructions for constructing your own built-in or freestanding closet.

If you have a dressing room or a small dressing table or you have the room to add one, you'll find plenty of ideas for organizing and decorating it.

Whether you choose just to add racks and hooks to your present closet or you decide to install a complete closet system with shelves, drawers, and rods, you're sure to be so pleased with the result that you'll wonder why you waited so long to do it.

Planning Closet Space

Specially created spaces can make a measurable difference
in keeping closets free from clutter

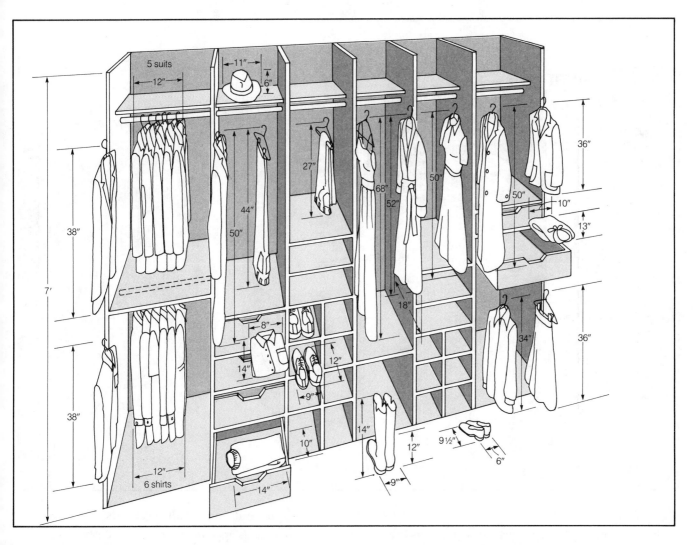

How much space do you need for clothing?

Most of us close our closet doors quickly—either to avoid
looking at the clutter or to stop all of those shoes, boxes,
coats, and caps in mid-tumble. And even when we take the
time to store things where they belong, there's never quite
enough space for everything.

Bringing order to a closet may be easier than you think.
With some planning, it's possible to have a closet that fits
your belongings, one with a variety of spaces for clothing
of different shapes and sizes, and one that doesn't crush
sweaters, crumple blouses, or wrinkle the hems of dresses.
It doesn't waste space and the rods don't sag.

Knowing the general dimensions of items in the basic
clothing categories can help you plan just how much room
to allow for each article. The drawing above gives measurements based on standards established by the American
Institute of Architects.

You can assume, for instance, that six men's shirts on
hangers will occupy a space at least 12 inches wide, 16
inches deep, and 38 inches high, and that a pair of women's
pumps of average size measures 6 by 9½ inches. But check
your own clothing against these measurements; you may
have bulkier jackets, longer hemlines, or larger shoes.

Wire hangers are usually 16 inches wide, wooden suit
hangers up to 21 inches wide, and tubular plastic or metal
ones about 17½ inches wide. Again, it's best to measure
your own hangers. Plastic, wood, or metal ones give your
clothing the best support.

A Closet System

Open shelves, drawers, and multilevel rods
work together to organize your clothes quarters

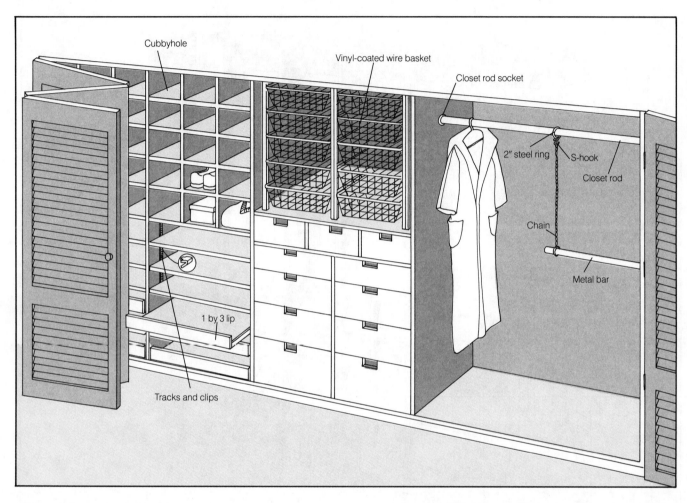

Open shelves

Shelves are probably the most versatile components in a closet system. They accommodate items in a wide variety of shapes and sizes (from ten-gallon hats to handkerchiefs); they keep stored items visible; and they're easy to install. And if you use an adjustable system of tracks and clips or tracks and brackets, shelves are also easy to rearrange.

Fir and pine are good choices for closet shelving; so are ¾-inch plywood and particleboard, especially if your shelves will be deeper than 12 inches. If you're planning a shelf longer than 4 feet (3 feet if it's particleboard), be sure to add a mid-span support.

For added interest—and convenience—use vertical dividers to form clusters of cubbyholes, or convert some of your shelves to pull-outs by adding standard drawer slides and lipped edges made from 1 by 3s.

Drawers, pull-outs, and multilevel rods

Simplify your dressing routine—and gain valuable floor space in the bedroom—by eliminating your bulky bureau and adding a new drawer system in the closet. If you want a built-in unit, construct a frame to accommodate drawers custom-made to desired dimensions. Or buy a modular set of drawers. For visible storage, try a system of vinyl-coated wire bins that glide in and out on their own framework.

In updated closets, the primary space-waster—the traditional single closet rod—has given way to multiple rods whose heights are determined by the owner's clothing. But you needn't make any major structural changes to convert your closet to multilevel rods. Just buy an adjustable suspension bar, or make one of your own from a metal bar or wood dowel, steel rings, S-hooks, and some lightweight chain (as shown).

Closet metamorphosis

Before the new storage system was installed (see inset), this all-too-typical closet broke virtually every rule for good closet design and organization. Its one long shelf was crammed with hats and handbags, books and bedding, while the extra foot of space between the shelf items and the ceiling above was totally unused. Clothes were jammed together on the one long closet rod, which was low enough to make long dresses and robes dust the floor, yet high enough to leave several feet of wasted space below jackets, skirts, and blouses. Impossible to vacuum, the closet floor was a dusty jumble of shoes, boots, handbags, and luggage.

With the new organizers in place, the closet holds everything it did before—and more—with room to spare. Five different levels of closet rods make sure that each item gets the space it needs. The closet floor is clear (and dust-free) now that shoes and handbags are lined up on shelves of their own. And, best of all, the owners were able to eliminate their bulky bedroom bureau—thanks to a stack of large-capacity closet draw-ers and some roomy open shelves for sweaters and other foldables. Closet interior: Just Closets.

Wall Closets

A custom design can double—even triple—
your closet's storage potential

Wardrobe at a glance

Many of us have closets we're only too glad to shut the door on. But this one offers a compartmentalized network so neat that it's actually pleasing to contemplate from the vantage point of one's bed at 6 A.M. (The slide-out tie rack just to the right of the mirrored center panel is shown more closely on page 48.)

When the bifold doors are closed, an expanse of mirrors not only aids grooming but also creates the illusion of doubled room depth. Interior design: Alan Lucas & Associates. Closet interior: The Minimal Space.

Planning ingenuity creates a closet for two

A little engineering carved ample storage for both his wardrobe and hers in a relatively compact space—leaving the rest of this bedroom serenely uncluttered. Baskets of vinyl-coated wire offer several advantages over traditional, and bulky, chests of drawers: they allow ventilation, they make it easier to find your favorite pullover, and they hide neatly behind the closet doors. Architect: N. Kent Linn. Interior design: Joan Simon. Closet interior: The Minimal Space.

Predawn efficiency

For many a commuter, every morning minute counts in the race to catch the train, bus, or carpool, and an efficiently arranged closet like this one can pare down dressing time and ease those important first decisions of the day. Thanks to the bifold doors, even sleep-filled eyes can take in most of the wardrobe at a glance. In the center of the closet, accessible from both sets of doors, are two rods offering double-decker storage for shirts, jackets, and slacks; at the far left, longer coats and robes hang at standard height. Shoe shelves eliminate floor clutter, and a stack of drawers and open shelves keeps folded shirts and other clothing in good order. Closet interior: Just Closets.

Cozy cache in a corner

Like the intricate honeycomb of a hard-working beehive, this remodeled high-and-narrow Victorian closet leaves scarcely a centimeter to chance disorder. New double-decker closet rods carry twice the freight of the original single one, and the newly installed bank of open shelves accommodates volumes of sweaters and other foldables without crush or confusion. Closet interior: Just Closets.

Walk-in Closets

Luxurious spots to shelter a wardrobe—some so spacious
they double as dressing rooms

Within easy reach of the bath

Housing your garments
adjacent to the bathroom can
save flurry and flutter as you
race the clock on weekday
mornings.

Such convenience was
feasible here without threat
of moisture damage to the
wardrobe. The spacious bathroom is well ventilated (a must
for this kind of arrangement),
and a sliding door seals off
the adjoining closet.

Lighting for the closet is
supplied by fluorescent
tubes above the cornices.
Architects: Designbank.

High-rise housing for clothing foldables

Good-looking enough to display books or collectibles, the wall unit at one end of this spacious walk-in is a private cache for quantities of foldable clothing. Cubbyholes at mid-level hold clear acrylic bins full of small items such as socks and lingerie. Double rods along one side of the closet, double shelves and a rod along the other, accommodate two extensive wardrobes neatly and without crowding. Design: Philip Emminger.

For clotheshorses, a spacious livery stable

Most walk-in closets are big enough to comfortably accommodate wardrobes for two people—even when each person makes frequent sartorial acquisitions. In this closet, there's space for floor-to-ceiling shoe shelves, a built-in chest of drawers, and a necktie rack. Double closet rods on either side offer an uncrowded abundance of raiment. And everything is easy to see—thanks to good indirect fluorescent lighting. Architect: Ron Yeo.

Open Closets

Honest, upfront clothes quarters to flaunt your finery

Letting it all hang out

Tucked under an eave, a man's collection of striped, plaid, and tattersall clothing makes an unobtrusive, tidy display that pleases the eye and detracts not a whit from the bedroom's striking design. During the day, skylights illuminate clothing colors; when the sun goes down, that function is performed by wall-mounted fixtures that look like jumbo dressing-table lights.

Above the closet is a compartment with sliding doors; to the left is a tall built-in unit with a white-enameled cabinet topping a dozen black-lacquered drawers. Architect: Wendell Lovett. Interior design: Suzanne Braddock.

Taking the hassle out of the morning

There's no wasted motion here. From the cup of freshly brewed coffee to the morning shave to the selection of the day's clothing, this open closet puts it all within arm's reach.

In addition, there's a built-in bureau to the left of the sink that holds sweaters and accessories, as well as towels for bathroom use. Recessed in the wall beside the door is a pull-down ironing board—right where it's needed. Interior design: Legallet-Trinkner Design Associates.

Two wardrobes separate bed and bath

Curved and compact, this room divider doubles as an open armoire for two people. Reminiscent of the voluptuous furniture styles of the 1930s, the closet curiosity has room for everything from brogues to silk dresses. The curved section offers open shelving, necktie pegs, a pull-out bin for laundry, and deep drawers of clear acrylic for small foldable items. Around the bend, facing the bathroom, there are additional nooks and crannies for towels and toiletries. Architect: Gary Allen.

Children's Closets

Organizing kids' clothes quarters for easy upkeep

Closet revamp encourages tidiness

With all his personal effects piled in a jumble, either on the floor or high up out of reach, it was hard for the eight-year-old owner of this closet to find things or put them away (see inset, right). But built-in shelves and drawers, plus an extra closet rod placed at just the right height for him, brought order out of frustrating chaos. At the same time, as with any well-planned closet remodel, space was cleared for storing at least twice as much. Closet interior: Just Closets.

Small girl's wardrobe makes a fetching display

Her mother's serendipitous shopping trips turned up unusual and elegant organizers for a five-year-old's wardrobe. Pretty hats and colorful dresses hang from an antique coat rack. Below that, a handsome wooden towel rack from a bath accessory boutique holds everyday play clothes. And, most imaginatively, her small-scale footwear lodges in a divided wicker desk tray originally designed to hold stationery. The entire arrangement makes a charming display in a small bedroom that has no built-in closet.

Organized for action

Though his toys may cover the floor most of the time, the right combination of drawers, shelves, and closet rods can make it easier for him to tidy up.

Vinyl-coated wire bins and adjustable shelving in the closet corral his shoes, sweaters, and soccer ball, while the shallow, open shelves in the chest at left keep his games and books visible—but neatly arranged. Two levels of rods in the closet make the most of the space and put the clothes on the lower level within easy reach. Interior design: Helen Kroeger, Interiors by Design.

Dressing Areas

Create a corner—or a luxurious separate room—
where you can retire to attire

Commodious corner closet

Designed for instant accessibility, this corner closet is composed of numerous compartments—glide-out trays for shoes, multiple shallow drawers for sweaters and lingerie, and two separate hanging areas, one for pants and dresses, the other for tops and jackets. There's even a hamper below the drawers.

Louvered doors that allow ventilation slide on tracks. One door is mirrored, which makes this compact area look larger. Architect: Mark Hajjar.

Reflections on the art of dressing

Look beyond the stunning hammered brass sink and brass-trimmed tile counter, and you're aware of something equally impressive reflected in the mirror: a spacious closet on the opposite wall of the dressing room proudly displays its beautifully stacked, stored, and suspended wares. Louvered for both good looks and good ventilation, its trifold doors hinge back to reveal an entire wardrobe. Architect: David Jeremiah Hurley. Interior design: Jois.

Plenty of doors and drawers

Behind the large double doors in this dressing room, you'll find a tidy double-rod clothes closet; behind the smaller doors are individual cubbyholes for as many as thirty pairs of shoes. Below the counter, built-in drawers of varying depths provide streamlined accommodation for folded items. Architect: Charles L. Howell.

Organizing Your Clothing & Footwear

Keep your wardrobe under control with these closet products and storage aids

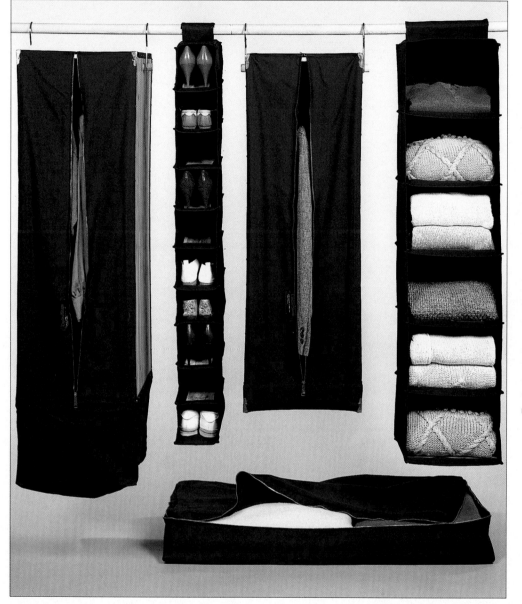

Garment bags give practical protection

Garment bags, like the ones shown at left, not only keep clothes clean and fresh-looking, but also can help organize the contents of your closet. They're especially useful for out-of-season or seldom-used clothing.

Made from fabric or from clear, colored, or patterned vinyl, the bags have front or side zippers for easy access and come in a wide range of sizes. Accessory bags with shelves for shoes, hats, handbags, sweaters, and other bulky items are also available.

You can find garment and accessory bags in the notions section of large department stores or in closet shops.

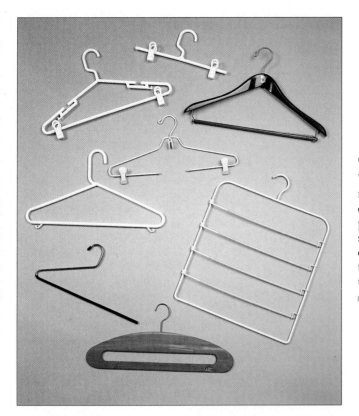

Good-bye to tangled wire hangers

Wire hangers, never meant for longtime use, crease slacks, misshape shoulders, and sag under the weight of heavy clothing. Replace them with sturdy hangers made from plastic, vinyl-coated wire, metal tubing, or wood. Designed specifically to keep garments looking crisp, these hangers come in a myriad of shapes and sizes. Before you shop, take a quick inventory of your closet to determine the types that will best meet your needs.

Footnote on shoe storage

Among the chief contributors to closet clutter are shoes. If you store them on the closet floor, or worse, under your bed, pulling out a matched pair can often be a challenge.

Ready-made shoe racks or boxes can provide an instant solution. Or, with some inexpensive materials, you can put together a custom rack of your own. Measure your closet space and count the pairs of shoes you need to store; then you'll know the size and shape rack to use.

Dressing Tables

Sitting down to all the accouterments of good grooming

Neatness counts

No tangle of cords and plugs mars the artful beauty of this carefully designed grooming area. Instead, holes drilled in the sides of the roomy drawers allow the hair blowers, curling irons, and other small appliances stored there to be plugged directly into a power strip under the counter. Only the cord emerges through the drawer's corner cut, which also serves as a drawer pull. A hole drilled in the corner of the counter carries the cords for the television and make-up mirror to the power strip.

Note how the accent stripes on the cabinetry echo those on the tile floor. Neon design: Wylie Mertz. Design and construction: Robert Nyden.

The romantic allure of wicker

An appealing beginning—and end—to each day are practically guaranteed at this charming little wicker vanity. Its simple, arched design catches the eye and may even divert attention from the clutter that all dressing tables inevitably collect. The unobtrusive glass shelves are easy to wipe clean. Furniture courtesy of de Benedictis Showrooms.

For today's fair lady, antique beauty

"The Fair each moment rises in her Charms/Repairs her Smiles, awakens ev'ry Grace/And calls forth all the Wonders of her Face." So wrote Alexander Pope early in the 18th century, addressing himself to the mysteries of a lady's toilette. For many of us, such marvelous transformations would be aided by an inspirational setting. Here's the very thing—an elegant Louis Philippe vanity with upholstered bench, both crafted of walnut. Lighting—essential to any dressing table—is stylishly supplied by smartly draped windows and a pair of lamps.

Organizing Your Accessories

Use baskets and barrels, hangers and holders
to arrange those all-important extras

Fold-up, slide-away tie ladder

The sides of this ladder rack swing up for easy access
to more than four dozen ties on six dowels. Once the tie
selection is made, the sides swing back down for compact storage. The entire unit slips in and out of the
closet on standard drawer slides. Design: The Minimal
Space.

Hidden jewelry storage

Tucked away in the back of a closet and concealed behind hanging garments is this clever hideaway for
jewelry. Built between the wall studs, the cabinet houses
eight fabric-lined, shallow drawers. For camouflage, the
outside of the cabinet door is painted the same color
as the rest of the closet wall, and the door opens by
means of a touch-latch. Design: Philip Emminger.

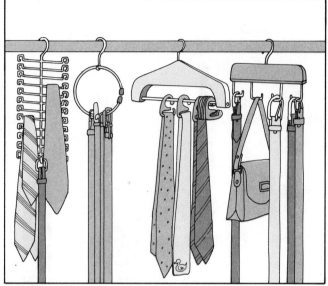

Put baskets and barrels to work as handy holders

Use baskets—wire or woven—to organize socks, lingerie, gloves, and scarves. Place them on closet shelves, tuck them into drawers, or suspend them from the closet ceiling.

Try a fiber drum, a small wine barrel, or an enameled metal drum to hold those tall, skinny items that are propped up precariously in the back corners of your closet: umbrellas, walking sticks, and sports equipment such as fishing rods, skis, baseball bats, and hockey sticks.

Hangers that major in accessories

Some smart-looking accessory holders, like the ones shown here, are designed to slip right over the closet rod. Available in the notions sections of most department stores or through mail-order catalogs, these specialty hangers hold belts, ties, scarves, handbags, or various combinations of accessories.

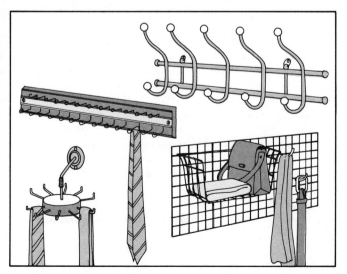

Wall hang-ups

One or more wall hang-ups in or near your closet can organize and display a variety of clothing accessories. Some simple plastic holders have an adhesive backing; others—fancy brass hooks, plastic or metal racks, and high-tech grid systems, for example—are screwed into the wall. For ties, there are collapsible racks or, if you prefer, revolving racks that bring favorites around at a touch.

Temporary & Portable Closets

Versatile storage pieces on hand when you need them—
and out of the way when you don't

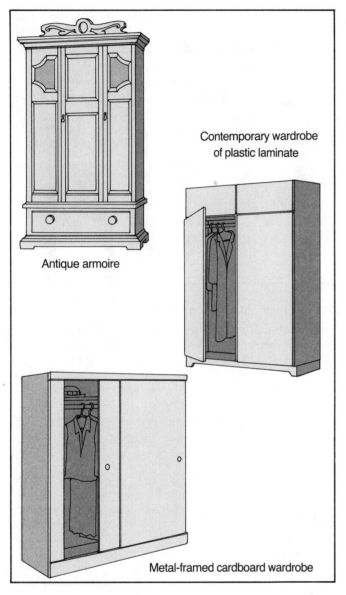

Contemporary wardrobe
of plastic laminate

Antique armoire

Metal-framed cardboard wardrobe

Freestanding wardrobes go where they're needed

Whether they're carved and mirrored antiques, sleek contemporary pieces of glossy plastic laminate, or inexpensive metal-framed cardboard units, freestanding wardrobes are as practical as ever. The original portable closets, they're a solution for bedrooms with little or no built-in closet space.

"Flying" closet

"Off-the-wall" closet

Suspended storage

Here are two commercially available hanging closets that are easy to carry and quick to install.

The "flying" closet is suspended on cotton webbing from two mounting hooks screwed into the ceiling joists. Garments hanging on the wooden closet rod are protected from dust by an attractive natural-color canvas awning.

The "off-the-wall" closet has a shelf built from natural-finish hardwood dowels with another dowel suspended below as a closet rod. The whole assembly hangs from natural-color cotton webbing straps that are attached to the wall studs. Closet designs: Richard Pathman.

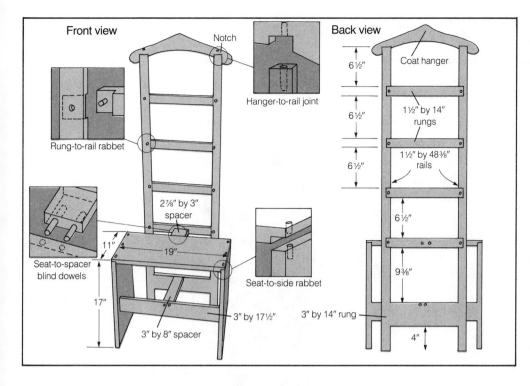

Front view

Notch

Hanger-to-rail joint

Rung-to-rail rabbet

2⅞" by 3" spacer

Seat-to-spacer blind dowels

11"

19"

17"

Seat-to-side rabbet

3" by 8" spacer

3" by 17½"

Back view

Coat hanger

6½"

6½"

6½"

1½" by 14" rungs

1½" by 48⅜" rails

6½"

9⅜"

3" by 14" rung

4"

A valet for clothes

This valet can help you lay out your clothes the night before or hold them for you after a hard day. Dowels and wood glue join parts. Equally spaced rabbeted rungs fit into dadoes in the back rails; the wider rung at the bottom is held with four dowels for stability. The seat is rabbeted.

Make the valet from hardwood except for the contoured hanger; buy a round-shouldered hardwood coat hanger at least ¾ inch thick; remove the hook and manufacturer's finish. Notch the hanger and glue it into place. Design: C. Stuart Welch.

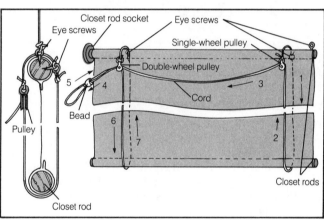

Closet rod socket

Eye screws

Eye screws

Single-wheel pulley

Double-wheel pulley

Cord

5

4

3

1

Bead

6

7

2

Pulley

Closet rods

Closet rod

Quick muslin closet on pulleys

Hung from the ceiling, this lightweight corner closet provides temporary storage in a minimum of space. Materials are simple: heavy muslin or duck canvas, thread, two wooden closet rods, closet rod sockets, #12 eye screws, ⅛-inch cotton shade cord, 3-penny finishing nails, a single- and a double-wheel ¾-inch pulley, a 3-inch cleat, and a large bead with a ¼-inch hole.

Cut the muslin into two pieces the desired height and width of the closet. The closet rods, cut into four pieces, slip into hems sewn at the top and bottom of each muslin piece. Drill holes in the upper rods for eye screws. Use cord and eye screws to fasten the fabric panels to ceiling joists; one end of each upper rod fits into a socket screwed or bolted to the wall (secure the rods with finishing nails). You can also fasten the panels to the floor to keep them taut. The drawing above shows how to rig the pull cord. Secure it to a cleat. Design: Diane McKenzie and Victor Budnik.

Adding a Built-in Closet

Constructing a closet where none existed before

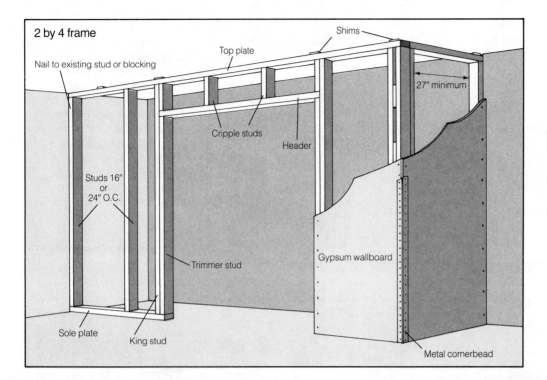

2 by 4 frame

Shims

Top plate

Nail to existing stud or blocking

27" minimum

Cripple studs

Header

Studs 16"
or
24" O.C.

Trimmer stud

Gypsum wallboard

Sole plate

King stud

Metal cornerbead

Two types of built-in closets

If you have the floor space and some basic skills, you can construct a built-in closet that looks as if it's been there since the beginning.

You can make the closet either with standard 2 by 4 framing and the wall covering of your choice, or by installing floor-to-ceiling plywood cabinets. For either, allow an inside depth of at least 27 inches.

To build a 2 by 4 frame, space the studs 16 or 24 inches on center. To frame the doorway, add the header and trimmer studs (be sure to have your doors—and the correct dimensions for the rough opening—on hand before you begin). Size the walls about ¼ inch less than ceiling height.

Once they're built, swing them into place, shim between the top plate and the ceiling joists, and nail the sole plate to the subfloor (but *not* inside the doorway). Cut out the sole plate between the trimmers. Anchor the end studs to existing wall studs or to blocking inserted between the studs. Next, add wallboard or another wall covering to match existing walls. Finally, hang the doors (see facing page).

Build plywood cabinets as multiple units (4 feet wide or less), carefully level and plumb them, and screw them to wall studs. Though not required, a kickbase at the bottom adds a custom touch.

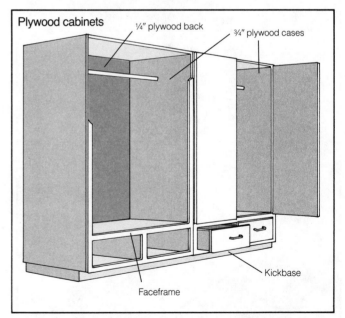

Plywood cabinets

¼" plywood back

¾" plywood cases

Faceframe

Kickbase

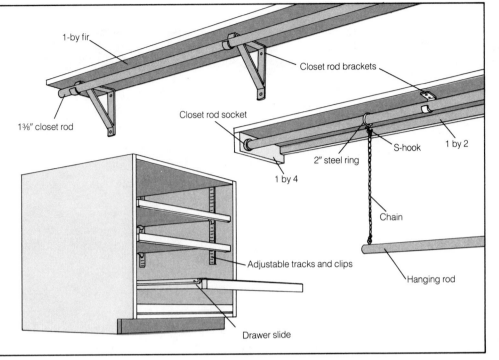

1-by fir

Closet rod brackets

1⅜" closet rod

Closet rod socket

2" steel ring

S-hook

1 by 2

1 by 4

Chain

Adjustable tracks and clips

Hanging rod

Drawer slide

A variety of closet rods and shelving

Closets with only one rod and one shelf often don't meet today's storage needs. With easy-to-install brackets, you can add a rod and shelf on an un-used wall. A simple hanging rod allows you to take advantage of the wasted space below short garments. Pull-out shelves in the corner of a closet can augment bureau space and keep your sweaters and other knits in shape.

Your local hardware store or closet shop can offer additional ideas for increasing your closet's storage capacity.

Closet door close-ups

If you're building a small closet that has ample clearance in front, a standard interior door may be all you need. But you may want to use one or two sets of either bifold or sliding doors. Both types are simple to install, as long as your rough opening is square.

A standard 2 by 4 closet frame requires some prep work before you can hang the doors. Add standard head and side jambs and trim the opening as you would any standard doorway.

Bifold doors move in metal tracks mounted to the bottom of the head jamb; pivots turn in top and bottom brackets, and a center guide at the top runs in the track.

Sliding doors run on rollers inside metal tracks; floor guides keep the doors in line below. Tracks are available to fit either ¾-inch plywood or standard 1⅜-inch interior doors.

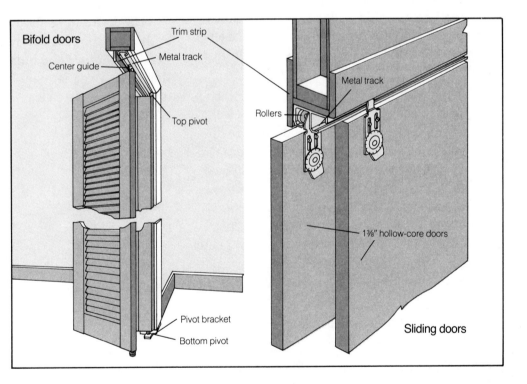

Bifold doors

Trim strip

Center guide

Metal track

Top pivot

Metal track

Rollers

1⅜" hollow-core doors

Pivot bracket

Bottom pivot

Sliding doors

Bathroom Storage

Of all the rooms in the house, the bathroom is usually the smallest—and the least seriously considered in terms of effective space planning. Yet today's bathrooms collect all kinds of paraphernalia, from hair blowers to hampers and from exercise equipment to magazines and books. Often, it all ends up in one big jumble.

To help you find your way, we've assembled a collection of photographs and drawings showing successful storage solutions tailored to the bathroom. Foremost among them is the bathroom vanity. Usually made from wood, vanities organize everything from cosmetics to cleaning supplies. Racks and hooks attached to the inside of doors can make the space even more efficient. In this section, we give instructions on how to build your own bathroom vanity. All you need are a few simple tools and some basic woodworking knowledge.

Medicine cabinets can do the work of several drawers or shelves. Some sit right above the sink; others fit between wall studs beside the sink.

Open shelving for towels, books, or even plants can take advantage of now-wasted space—above toilets, between the studs, or in corners. If moisture isn't a problem and you have the floor space, consider moving in a small piece of furniture, such as a bookcase or an attractive wood chest.

Small appliance caddies or a grid system that's attached to the wall can organize your vanity top in a jiffy, as can a soap dish and toothbrush holder. And a shower caddy can place soap and shampoo just where you need them—in the shower.

Think carefully about what you use frequently in the bathroom as you're planning your storage needs. Whether you build your own units or buy them ready-made, your best resources are your imagination and a clear understanding of your needs.

Space-makers

Maximizing storage around the sink

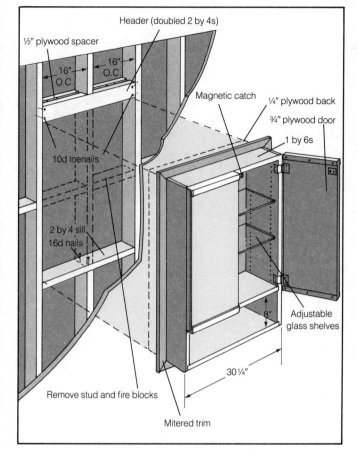

Header (doubled 2 by 4s)
½" plywood spacer
16" O.C.
16" O.C.
Magnetic catch
¼" plywood back
¾" plywood door
1 by 6s
10d toenails
2 by 4 sill
16d nails
Adjustable glass shelves
8"
Remove stud and fire blocks
30¼"
Mitered trim

Built-in bathroom cabinet

A built-in cabinet recessed between wall studs can provide needed storage without taking over the room. Though you could fit a very narrow cabinet between studs, in most cases you'll have to remove part of one middle stud and reframe the opening.

First, locate the studs in the area and check for any wiring or plumbing. If all is clear, mark the inside edges of the studs you'll keep; also mark top and bottom lines at the height you want the cabinet, adding 3½ inches at the top and 1½ inches at the bottom for the new header and sill.

Cut an opening through the wall covering along the lines. Knock off any fire blocks. With a handsaw, cut the middle stud squarely and carefully pry it away from the wall covering on the other side. Make the header as shown and toenail it inside the opening. Cut a 2 by 4 sill to the same length and nail it in place.

Build the cabinet frame from 1 by 6 lumber, making it ¼ inch less in height and width than the size of the opening. Nail on a ¼-inch plywood back. Drill holes for shelf pegs or pins, add doors, and finish.

Position the cabinet in the opening, shimming it level and plumb, and nail it to the framing. Attach the trim, mitering the corners, and then add shelves.

No wasted space under this sink

Most bathroom cabinets have one large space under the sink, often stuffed with layers of bottles, sponges, bath toys, and packages of toilet tissue—none of which is easy to reach or see.

One simple solution is to build drawers that wrap around the sink and its plumbing. Each drawer has a curving rear, cut from 18-gauge sheet metal and fastened to the sides and bottom with sheet-metal screws. Design: Bill Ridenour.

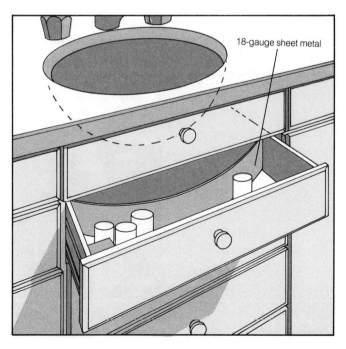

18-gauge sheet metal

Cabinetry: The "Inside" Story

Clutter-swallowing helpers that hide behind closed cabinet doors

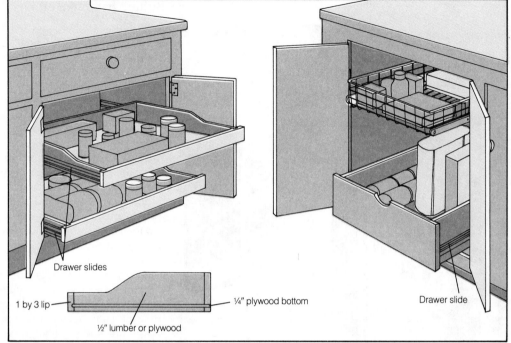

Drawer slides

1 by 3 lip

½" lumber or plywood

¼" plywood bottom

Drawer slide

Back-of-the-door bonanza

A wood or vinyl-coated wire storage rack mounted to the inside of a cabinet door can help you organize soaps, shampoos, and other cosmetics, as well as bathroom cleaning supplies.

Problem-solving pull-outs

There's no need to grope around in your bathroom cabinets in search of that extra tube of toothpaste or the bubble bath you got last Christmas. With pull-outs like the ones shown here, bath supplies glide right out for easy access. Available in plastic, wood, and regular or vinyl-coated wire, pull-outs can be installed on full-extension drawer slides or on their own special framework.

Not-so-lazy Susans

These hard-working storage-go-rounds help keep bathroom paraphernalia from finding its way into the far reaches of your cabinetry. Single-level or tiered, a lazy Susan rotates so that everything you store is visible and accessible. Be sure to measure your cabinet carefully—allowing for drainpipe clearance, if necessary—before you buy or build one of these organizers.

These cabinets put away plenty

Imported from Germany, this plastic laminate bath cabinetry carries all the soaps, cleansers, lotions, creams, and scents you'll need for some time to come. The gleaming chrome towel rack swings out of the way to allow easy access to the spacious undersink compartment; the cabinet on the left features swivel-out trays in various sizes. Cabinetry courtesy of European Kitchens & Baths.

Mirror magic

Concealed behind a mirrored door, these under-the-counter pull-outs glide into view when you need them. Two shallow and two deep drawers hold cosmetics, towels, and cleaning products. Doors operate with touch-latches. Interior design: Helen Kroeger, Interiors by Design.

Cabinetry of Wood

The traditional raw material of the cabinetmaker's art,
shown here in designs that are far from ordinary

**Old wood adds
warmth to a new bath**

Antique cabinet, fitted
with modern basins, takes
on a new life in this older
home's remodeled master
bathroom. Capacious
drawers in the center section hold towels and toilet
articles. There's also plenty
of undersink storage at
either end. Architect:
William B. Remick.

Hollywood glamour, right at home

Curving cabinetry and theatrical make-up lights add star quality to this sleek sink and storage area. The mirrored panels at either end of the unit are actually mirror-faced doors for twin medicine cabinets. And below the sink, a cupboard and bank of drawers offer roomy recesses for tucking away towels, lotions, and other accouterments of glamorous grooming. Architects: Olsen/ Walker. Cabinet design: The Butt Joint.

Orderly without, organized within

There's nothing trendy about this bathroom storage wall and sink counter. The attractive traditional-style wood cabinetry and a mirrored medicine cabinet just look great and do their job—keeping bath necessities and even clothing in their proper place—while giving the whole room a pleasing sense of order. Who could ask for more? When open to view, the drawers and doors disclose a wealth of storage organization, including a roomy set of wooden pull-outs. Design: Dennis O'Connor.

Cabinetry of Plastic Laminate

The sleek, chic European imports
are a bold new bath-storage option

**Plastic pizzazz,
Italian-style**

From the ultra-modern
approach of northern Italian
design comes this factory-
molded sculptural elegance
for the bathroom. The clever
countertop towel rack whim-
sically plays with terrycloth
tones, creating vertical stripes
that balance the horizontal
strokes of navy blue on the
wall above. Drawers and
cabinets are anything but
boring—they're concave or
convex; they can be pulled
or swiveled. And even the
vanity stool stands for more
than just plain seating—it
stores things, too. Cabinetry
courtesy of Dahl Designs.

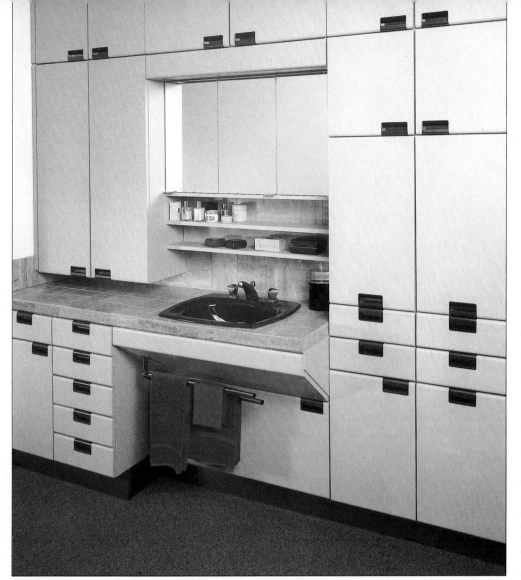

Wall-covering cabinetry

This German cabinetry puts every square inch of a bathroom wall to work—with precision. The fine-lined pattern on drawers and cabinet doors provides an interesting texture that's resistant to fingerprints, as well. Behind the beautiful façade are cleverly designed interiors to accommodate everything from cosmetics to laundry. (You can peek behind the doors on pages 57 and 71.) Cabinetry courtesy of European Kitchens & Baths.

Not corners, but curves

This sand and charcoal-colored cabinetry presents a rounded look that's a refreshing contrast to the harsher, predominantly angular environment of many bathrooms. So there are no handles to interrupt the smooth façade, all cabinets open with touch-latches. The bottom cabinet on the far side (shown open) features a swing-out towel rack. Cabinetry courtesy of Dahl Designs.

Open Shelves

Out-in-the-open storage puts towels
and other bright bath supplies on display

**Tubside art
enhances the bath**

Surely one of the most
sumptuous of life's simple
pleasures is a good, hot
soak in a bubbly bath. To
enrich the experience,
this bathroom provides
a colorful gallery of
miniature folk art for
bathtime viewing. Be-
sides display space, the
handsome cedar shelves
offer storage for bright
towels, and even for a
few books. Architect:
William Abbott.

Towels sit high up in brassy splendor

In days gone by, this vintage piece held luggage overhead
in a cramped train compartment. Today, in a crowded
bathroom, it keeps extra towels out of the way, yet
within reach. Its brass mesh shelf and filigree framing
are a treat to view from underneath. Design: Rand
Hughes.

Greenhouse windows offer shelf space

Greenhouse popouts, available from building-supply and home-improvement centers, can provide extra space and daylight, as well as wide views of the leafy world outside. At the same time, they offer attractive shelf space for both practical and decorative items. Since the room faces a shady corner of the garden, there's no worry that sunlight might fade the towels. Design: Woody Dike.

Mini-library for private browsing

Many people appreciate the privacy bathrooms afford for reading in undistracted solitude. Here, a colorful collection of paperbacks offers not only food for thought, but hospitality and decorative cheer as well. You'll find more ideas for bathroom libraries on pages 72–73. Design: Jeanne Kleyn.

Graceful niche for bath necessities

An arched alcove, traversed by a single glass shelf, creates open wall storage with a clean and airy feeling. The rectangular opening just below houses a fluorescent light behind a frosted glass panel; more glass functions as sliding doors for the base cabinet.

Under the window, a laundry hamper disguises itself as a simple ledge when its lid is closed. Architects: Ted Tanaka and Frank Purtill.

Linen Closets

Orderly accommodation for the bulk of your bed and bath needs

Closet chic

Clean-as-a-whistle white shelving etches a crisp border around stacked sheets and towels in this walk-in linen closet.

Derived from an industrial design, these vinyl-coated wire shelves are available for the home through specialty shops, interior designers, and home centers. Besides their look of high-tech sophistication, they offer other advantages: good air circulation, light weight, quick installation, and easy access to their contents. Architect: John Galbraith.

Sleek exterior, hard-working interior

One basic aim of good storage design is an everything-in-place look that's gentle on the eyes. When all its doors and drawers are closed, this floor-to-ceiling storage wall blends unobtrusively into its all-white bathroom surroundings—only the glistening brass hardware calls attention to its function. Behind the cabinet doors, colorful linens are neatly arranged on lipped, pull-out shelves. Architects: Fisher/Friedman Associates.

Storing linens for just one room

Often, each bedroom has its own linens—sheets and blankets that coordinate with the decor and fit the bed in the room. What better place to store them than in the bedroom itself? Here, a narrow cabinet at the end of a wall system (see page 21 for another view) is fitted with shelves deep enough to accommodate pillows, sheets, and a quilt. Interior design: Patricia Whitt Designs.

Medicine Cabinets

Handy, high-style housing for home remedies
and prescriptions, first-aid supplies and cosmetics

Pops open at a touch

Just give this medicine cabinet door a little push and it'll pop right open— thanks to the convenient touch-latch. Since the door opens upward, you'll want to position the cabinet low enough for adults' convenience, but high enough to prevent bumped foreheads. Cabinet courtesy of Plus Kitchens.

Low-lying cabinets leave room for a view

For many of us, the first sight of the day, as we splash cold water on our faces, is somewhat less inspiring than a gentle garden view. But as this thoughtful arrangement makes clear, the traditional over-the-sink mirror is not compulsory. Here, you can have it both ways: twin medicine cabinets with mirrored sliding doors are recessed into the backsplash area, leaving space for a window above one sink and for a mirror above the other. Architects: Ted Tanaka and Frank Purtill.

Prescription for storage

Built in between the wall studs, this wooden medicine chest is compact yet roomy, with storage space on the inside of the cabinet door as well as on the interior shelves. Small-diameter wooden dowels keep door-stored items in place. Design: Jeanne Kleyn.

Cabinet puts corner to work

Tucked into a corner between the sink and bathtub, this jumbo medicine cabinet holds cosmetics, remedies, and bath supplies for the whole family. Below it is a tip-out laundry hamper (you see it open on page 70). Architect: William B. Remick.

Bathroom Organizers

Caddies, soap dishes, and hampers keep
bathroom counters and shelves clean and orderly

Shower heads have hang-ups, too

No longer do you have to
perch your shower sup-
plies precariously on a
windowsill or tub ledge.
These shower caddies,
which hang from a shower
head, hold shampoo,
soap, and washcloths.
Open shelves allow arti-
cles to drain and dry be-
tween showers.

Catchalls for containers and appliances

Slanted compartments of
the clear acrylic appliance
caddy hold hair dryers
and curling irons; its
straight section puts
combs and brushes within
easy reach. The caddy can
sit on a countertop or
hang on a wall.

   Vinyl-coated wire or
plastic baskets, like the
one shown, corral items of
different shapes and sizes,
reducing bathroom clutter
and eliminating last-
minute hassles.

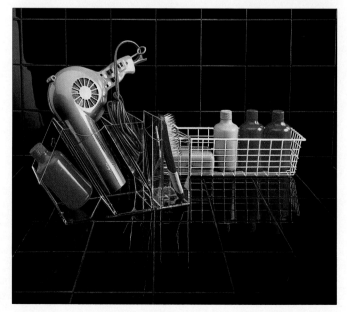

An array of soap dish designs

Even the lowly bar of soap rises to new heights in today's distinctive soap dishes. Whether your decor is starkly modern or traditional, your choices range from clear acrylic to colorful plastic to clear-finished wood. If your dish doesn't have drainage holes or slats, you can add a ribbed or spiked plastic insert specially designed for this purpose.

Movable hampers—and they're washable, too

These two alternatives to the traditional bulky bathroom hamper are made from fast-drying nylon. The hanging hamper can collect clothing for a few days on a wall hook or at the end of a shower bar. It's available in a range of colors to complement almost any bathroom decor. The larger laundry bag slips onto a lightweight metal-tubing frame.

Hampers

A fresh, new look at those bathroom basics

Hatch lifts up to catch clothing

The sturdy fir deck around this bathtub provides more than just good-looking surroundings for a sudsy soak. It also makes efficient use of the space between the tub and a wall by offering a roomy built-in laundry hamper. When the lid is closed, the spot doubles as a dressing bench. Design: James Fey.

Tip-out bin for a tight spot

In this bathroom, a tip-out laundry bin takes clever advantage of the corner between the sink and bathtub. It serves its purpose smoothly in a tight-cornered room where a conventional freestanding hamper would only be in the way. Architect: William B. Remick.

For towel-tossing

Flip open this sleek tilt-down cabinet door and you find a laundry hamper just waiting for you to play doff-and-toss. The vinyl-coated wire basket lifts out so that after you've flung your clothing and towels into it, you can carry the whole works over to the washer. Cabinetry courtesy of European Kitchens & Baths.

Laundry collection point

With a hamper between these double sinks, dirty towels need never clutter the towel bars or floor. A finger reveal in the drawer top lets you pull the bin out and tilt it slightly. It's deep enough to hold a load of wash. Interior design: Teri Rickel, Dovetail Interior Design.

A Very Private Library

Racks to display your current collection
of periodicals and paperbacks

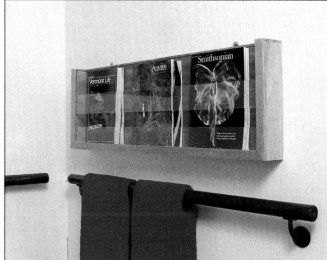

Three-in-one wall unit

With a small bathroom, you can't afford to waste even the awkward space between the toilet and the adjacent wall. The handy redwood unit shown here offers a lot in a limited area: a shallow yet roomy cabinet for extra soap and paper products, a tissue holder, and a very simple magazine rack. (Magazines stand on top of the supply cabinet and are held in place by two redwood trim strips.) Design: Marshall Design-Built.

See-through strips let magazine covers brighten bath

In this wall rack, magazines are held in place by two strips, as in the rack shown on the left. But instead of redwood, the strips here are made of clear acrylic to give a sleek, contemporary look—and to let colorful magazine covers show through. The rest of the unit is simply a shallow, three-sided wooden box. Design: John Matthias.

Cabinet creates a paperback perch

Spanning a toilet alcove, the top of this wooden medicine cabinet is home to a collection of paperback books. Open shelves are an appealing—though often overlooked—option for bathroom storage; pages 62–63 show several other ways in which creative homeowners and designers have put them to work. Design: The Butt Joint.

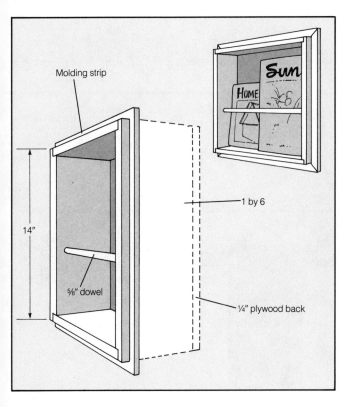

Molding strip

14"

⅝" dowel

1 by 6

¼" plywood back

Between-the-studs box library

This recessed rack for reading matter is a simple box that fits snugly between two wall studs. Since wall studs are usually 16 or 24 inches apart (center to center), your box library will probably need to be 14½ or 22½ inches wide; 14 inches is a convenient height for it. Locate the studs, measure and mark your wall carefully, then remove only enough wallboard to accommodate the box. (Pick a location for your box library where you won't run into electrical wiring and plumbing lines inside the wall.)

Use fir 1 by 4s or 1 by 6s for the box frame (1 by 6s will add extra depth, but they'll stick out slightly from the wall). Before assembling the frame drill shallow holes in the side pieces to hold a ⅝-inch dowel (see illustration). Assemble the frame and add a ¼-inch plywood back. Slide the unit into the wall cutout, and side-nail the box to one or both wall studs. Add molding strips or wood trim around the box to hide the rough edges and give a built-in look. Finally, finish the unit with enamel, varnish, or polyurethane. Design: John Schmid.

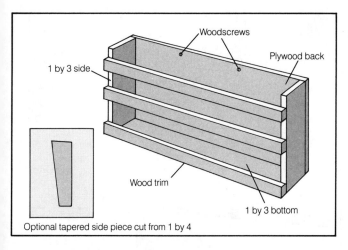

Woodscrews

Plywood back

1 by 3 side

Wood trim

1 by 3 bottom

Optional tapered side piece cut from 1 by 4

No-frills wall rack

This simple wall rack is remarkably easy to build. Cut two side pieces and a bottom piece from pine or fir 1 by 3s, and cut a back from ¼-inch or ⅜-inch plywood. Assemble the rack, then nail ¼-inch-thick strips of wood trim across the front to keep magazines and books in place. Finally, drive two woodscrews through the back of the rack and into the wall studs and apply a paint, varnish, or polyurethane finish. The unit illustrated is approximately 12 inches high and 20 inches wide, but these dimensions can be adjusted to suit your needs and wall space.

If you must get fancy, build the rack with tapered side pieces (cut from 1 by 4s) so your reading matter tilts forward for easier access.

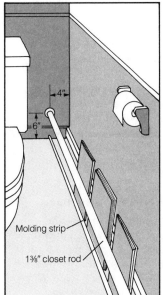

4"

6"

Molding strip

1⅜" closet rod

Closet rod corrals magazines

A 1⅜-inch wooden closet rod, mounted 4 inches out from the wall and 6 inches above the floor, can keep magazines rounded up in what would otherwise be wasted space. A molding strip attached to the floor (as shown) will keep magazines from sliding forward. If your bathroom floor tends to collect water, add a narrow wooden platform (with the molding strip on top) to keep your reading matter high and dry.

Towel Hang-ups

A whole raft of racks, rails, rods, and rings that you can buy or build

Redwood and towels—two ways to go

Here's a pair of easy-to-make variations on the basic towel bar theme. One is a no-nonsense rail; the other is a fancier, and slightly more challenging, two-rung rack.

The rustic rail is made from a long redwood 2 by 2 held out from the wall by 4½-inch-long end blocks made of 2 by 3s. Lag screws 3½ inches long attach the rail to the end blocks; the end blocks are attached to wall studs with 5½-inch-long lag screws. (Be sure to find the wall studs before you decide on a length for your rail.) If lag screw heads seem too rustic, you can countersink them and cover them with dowel plugs.

For the two-rung rack, use 1½-inch wooden rods and redwood, fir, or pine 2 by 12s. From the 2 by 12s, cut two curved wall mounts like the one shown; smooth them with a rasp and sandpaper. Drill shallow holes in the mounts to support the rods, positioning the lower rod in front of the upper one, as shown. Two screws fasten each mount to the wall studs. (Again, determine the length of your rack after you've located the wall studs.)

A bathroom's humid climate can be tough on unfinished wood, so be sure to protect your new towel bars with several coats of polyurethane finish or penetrating resin.

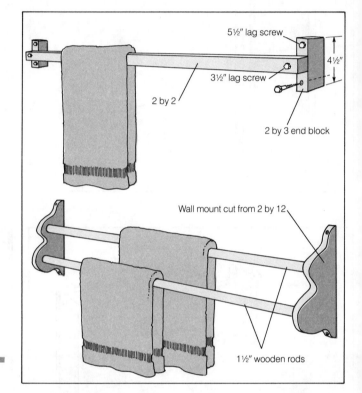

5½" lag screw

4½"

3½" lag screw

2 by 2

2 by 3 end block

Wall mount cut from 2 by 12

1½" wooden rods

Recessed towel bar

Located just below and slightly to the side of your bathroom sink, this 1 by 2 bar allows you to grab a towel without having to grope for it. Make the pocket 2½ inches deep and line its surfaces to match the cabinet facing. The bar itself is inset ½ inch from the cabinet front. Architect: Henry Wood.

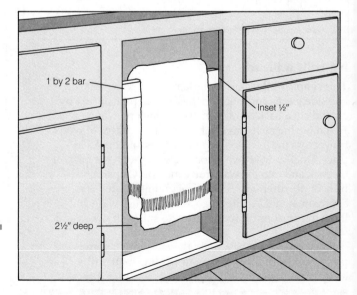

1 by 2 bar

Inset ½"

2½" deep

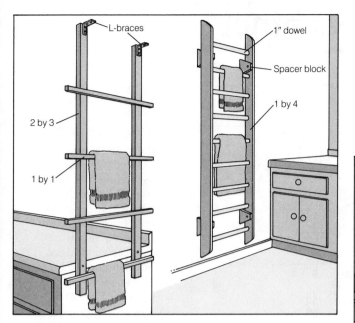

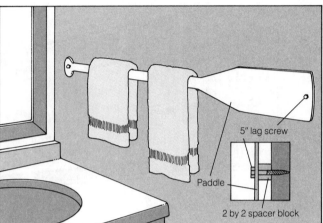

The lowdown on ladders

Floor-to-ceiling towel ladders make the most of narrow spaces. They're also very easy to build.

Simply nail 1 by 1 strips to the front edges of two parallel 2 by 3 uprights. Or recess 1-inch dowels into matching holes in two parallel 1 by 4 uprights; glue the dowels in place and clamp them securely until dry. Fasten your ladder to the floor and/or ceiling with L-braces (be sure to allow at least ¼ inch between the top of the ladder and the ceiling for clearance) or attach it to spacer blocks that you've screwed into wall studs.

Redwood is an excellent material for towel holders because it's moisture-resistant. Hardwoods are also good but are somewhat more expensive. Protect the wood with a polyurethane finish or penetrating resin.

This paddle stays high and dry

This sleek 5-foot towel bar is actually a canoe paddle that was purchased for under $10 at a marine supply store. It's attached to the wall studs with two 5-inch-long lag screws that run through holes drilled in the paddle and in two spacer blocks cut from a 2 by 2. Several coats of clear marine varnish make this unusual towel bar "weatherproof."

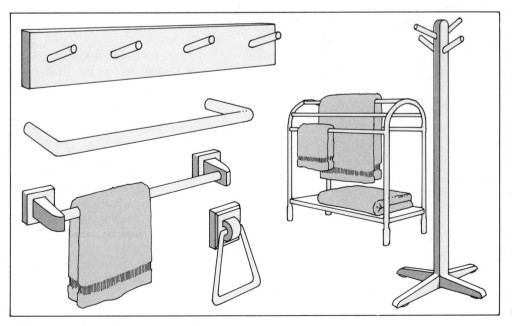

Ready-made racks

If you'd rather buy a towel rack than build one, you'll find a large selection of ready-mades. Standard bars and rings, sold individually or as components in matching accessory sets, are available in a wide variety of materials—from brass to chrome, from oak to plastic. Another option is a wall rack with wooden pegs or brass hooks.

If you have floor space to spare, consider a freestanding rack, such as a towel tree or a floor stand with room for both hanging and folded towels.

Building a Bathroom Cabinet

In remodeled bathrooms and in new ones,
cabinets add both style and efficiency

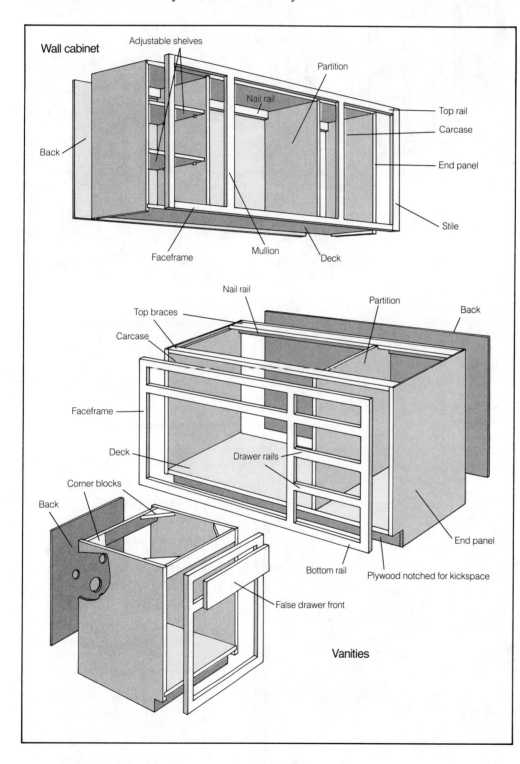

Wall cabinet

Adjustable shelves

Partition

Nail rail

Top rail

Carcase

End panel

Back

Stile

Faceframe

Mullion

Deck

Nail rail

Top braces

Partition

Back

Carcase

Faceframe

Deck

Drawer rails

Corner blocks

End panel

Back

Bottom rail

Plywood notched for kickspace

False drawer front

Vanities

Building the basic box

Basically, cabinets are boxes fitted with drawers, doors, and shelves. Called carcases, the boxes, usually made from plywood, are then fitted with solid-lumber faceframes that hide the plywood edges.

The carcases of both vanities and wall cabinets are composed of end panels, a bottom (called a deck), a back, and, often, interior partitions. Ends, partitions, and decks are usually made from ¾-inch plywood and the back from ¼-inch plywood. Typically, vanities are 32 inches high (including the countertop) and 21 inches deep.

Wall cabinets have plywood top panels; vanities are fitted with top braces, which both square up the case and serve as nailers for the countertop. Small vanities sometimes have flat, triangular corner blocks for the same purpose. Nail rails aid in attaching the cabinet to the wall.

Rabbets and dadoes make strong connections for carcase parts, but basic butt joints work well, too. Use glue and nails or screws to secure the joints.

Usually, faceframes are made from 1-by hardwood joined with glue and dowels. Attach the faceframe with finishing nails.

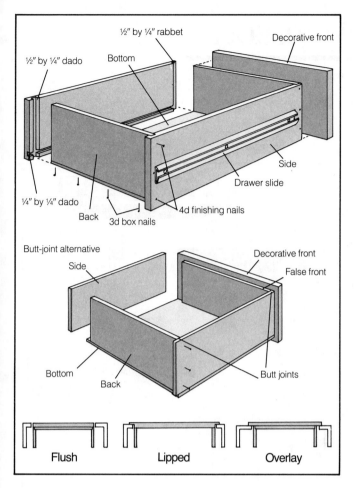

½" by ¼" rabbet

½" by ¼" dado

Bottom

Decorative front

½" by ¼" dado

Side

Drawer slide

¼" by ¼" dado

Back

3d box nails

4d finishing nails

Butt-joint alternative

Side

Decorative front

False front

Bottom

Back

Butt joints

Flush   Lipped   Overlay

Designing drawers

Drawers come in three basic styles: flush, lipped, or overlay (see drawing at left). A *flush* drawer lines up even with the front of the cabinet; on a *lipped* drawer, part of the front projects slightly past; the entire front of an *overlay* drawer sits outside the faceframe. It's easiest to build drawers with a false front, which allows you to build a basic box, hang it, and then align the decorative front exactly.

Make the drawers from ½-inch plywood or pine; the fronts are made from either ¾-inch plywood or solid lumber. Drawer bottoms are typically ¼-inch plywood or hardboard.

Drawers are stronger if the pieces are joined with dadoes and rabbets, but simple butt joints will work, too. Make the box height the same as the opening minus ¼ inch. Drawer width is also nominally the opening minus ¼ inch—subtract extra for any side-mounted drawer slides. Generally, box depth is ¼ inch less than the depth of the recess, unless your drawer slides require additional space in back.

Be sure when you're measuring box depth to allow for your front style: measure flush drawers from the back edge of the faceframe, add ⅜ inch for lipped drawers, and measure from the cabinet front for overlay drawers.

For trouble-free drawer action, metal ball-bearing drawer slides are the best choice. Be sure to leave sufficient clearance for them.

Building doors

Study any cabinet door and you'll most likely find it's either a flat plywood door or a frame-and-panel style.

A *flat* door is the simplest to make, whether it's flush, lipped, or overlay. For best results, cut the door from ¾-inch lumber-core plywood.

The rails and stiles of *frame-and-panel* doors are made from 1-by or 4/4 lumber; panels can be ¼-inch plywood or edge-joined ½-inch lumber. The easiest type to make is a plywood panel that fits into a rabbet in the back of the frame. Raised-bevel (see at right) and square-shoulder panels are made from ½-inch plywood or ½-inch solid stock.

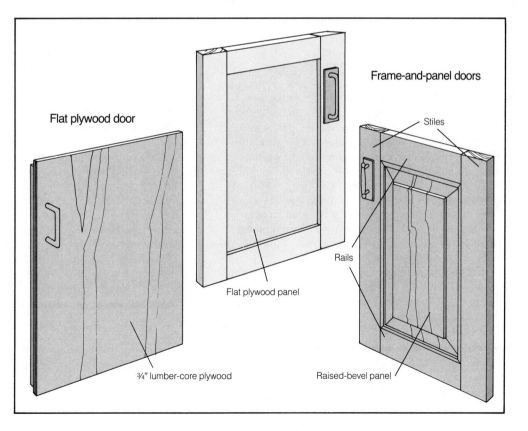

Flat plywood door

Flat plywood panel

¾" lumber-core plywood

Frame-and-panel doors

Stiles

Rails

Raised-bevel panel

Small Appliances & Accessories

Here are several solutions to the problem of where to stash your grooming gadgets, plus some holders for tissue and toothbrushes

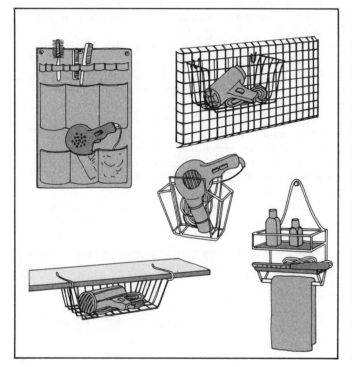

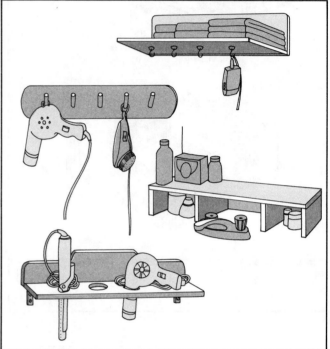

Ready-made solutions to appliance storage problems

The popularity and proliferation of personal-grooming gadgets have put bathroom storage at an even greater premium. We have electric toothbrushes and water jets; blow dryers, curling irons, and electric rollers; shavers, tweezers, complexion brushes, and manicure machines—but how can we keep them all organized and within reach?

Storage aids not designed specifically for small appliances can be easily pressed into service: consider shower caddies (remember that they can be hung on an open wall as well as over a shower head), wall-mounted vinyl pouches (often sold as closet organizers), and under-shelf baskets of vinyl-coated wire.

Perhaps the most flexible approach to small appliance storage is a vinyl-coated wire grid system. Appliances with hanging loops can be suspended on hooks; those without loops can be stored in the bins and baskets that are available as components of such systems.

Some improvised solutions

If your small grooming appliances have hanging loops, then simple hooks or pegs are all you'll need for storage. Put together a taproom rack from a redwood backing strip and some brass hooks or hardwood-dowel pegs; or simply screw cuphooks to the underside of a bathroom shelf.

If you'd rather not hang your appliances, consider a narrow shelf with carefully measured holes drilled through it to form holsters for your curling iron, your shaver, or the nozzle of your blow dryer. For several large or heavy appliances, try a wider shelf running the length of the sink counter and 6 to 8 inches above it; support the shelf with wood blocks spaced to form counter-level cubbyholes for cosmetics and grooming aids. For moisture protection, finish wood shelves with enamel or two coats of clear polyurethane.

Tissue holders to buy or build

Tissue holders are available in a wide variety of styles and materials—from traditional steel or ceramic holders with spring-loaded inserts, to high-tech plastic models in bright colors, to costly antique reproductions in solid brass. But tissue holders are also very easy to make, and the handsome wooden ones shown here are fine examples.

The two ends of a teak ship's rail (from a marine supply store) make a very stylish holder. Just drill a small hole in the inside edge of each piece to accommodate a spring-loaded insert (available at most hardware stores), and add shims, if necessary, to increase wall clearance. (Remember that a new roll of tissue is about 5 inches in diameter, so the insert's center must be at least $2\frac{3}{4}$ inches from the wall.)

The horizontal-dowel holder substitutes a 1-inch dowel for the spring-loaded insert. Cut two end pieces (in any shape you like) from a fir 2 by 6. Then drill a 1-inch-diameter hole halfway through one end piece and a corresponding hole completely through the other end piece (so the dowel can be removed). Allow at least $4\frac{1}{2}$ inches clearance between end pieces (that's the width of a standard roll).

With the vertical-dowel holder, the tissue roll stands on end. Use scrap blocks of fir, oak, or redwood and a 5-inch-long $1\frac{1}{4}$-inch dowel. Assemble the pieces (as shown) with woodscrews and glue.

Mounting tissue holders may require some patience. Some end pieces are easier to mount if they are first bridged by a backing piece which is then attached directly to the wall. Try to anchor a holder to a wall stud; if that's not feasible, use expanding anchors or toggle bolts.

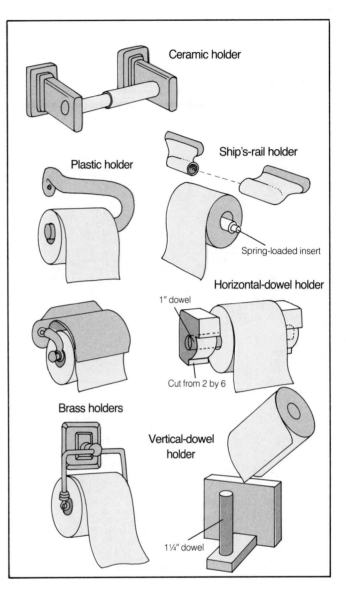

Ceramic holder

Plastic holder

Ship's-rail holder

Spring-loaded insert

Horizontal-dowel holder

1" dowel

Cut from 2 by 6

Brass holders

Vertical-dowel holder

$1\frac{1}{4}$" dowel

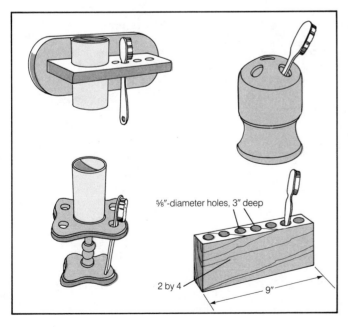

⅝"-diameter holes, 3" deep

2 by 4

9"

Dental details: a brush-up course

Choose one of the many commercially available toothbrush holders—freestanding or wall-mounted, with tumbler or without—or make one of your own from a scrap block of oak.

Begin with a 9-inch-long 2 by 4. Into one edge, drill eight ⅝-inch-diameter holes, each 3 inches deep (see illustration). Smooth the entire holder with fine sandpaper. Finish the wood with two coats of clear polyurethane to protect it from the humid bathroom climate—and from dripping toothbrushes.

Index